English Language
Learning Resource

Speak English in 10 days

Download audio of this book at:
www.SpeakEnglishIn10Days.com
(Passcode: ROLL)

英語
学習教材

10日間で英語を話そう

この本の音声はこちらからダウンロード出来ます

www.SpeakEnglishIn10Days.com

(パスコード: ROLL)

Legal Disclaimer

This Multimedia Learning Resource is the property of the author Boris Poludo. It is for your own use only. Reproduction and distribution are illegal. No part of this publication shall be reproduced, stored in a retrieval system, or transmitted in any form or by any means (electronic, mechanical, photocopying, recording, translated) or used to produce derivative works or otherwise, without written permission from the author. All the information in this Multimedia Learning Resource is meant as educational material – we do not guarantee the results or take any responsibility over the results created by implementing any of the strategies, instructions and recommendations provided in this book. It is provided with the understanding that the author and the publisher are not engaged in rendering legal, accounting, or other professional advice. If legal advice or other professional assistance is required, the services of a competent professional should be sought.

I Boris Poludo do not accept any responsibility or any liabilities resulting from the actions of any parties involved with this derivative work. While all attempts have been made to verify information provided in this publication, neither the Author nor the Publisher assume any responsibility for errors, omissions, or contrary interpretation of the subject matter herein. This publication is not intended for use as a source of legal or accounting advice. The Author and Publisher want to stress that the information contained herein may be subject to varying state and/or local laws or regulations. All users are advised to retain competent counsel to determine what state and/or local laws or regulations may apply to the user's particular business. The purchaser or reader of this publication assumes responsibility for the use of these materials and information. Adherence to all applicable laws and regulations, federal, state, and local, governing professional licensing, business practices, advertising, and all other aspects of doing business in Canada or any other jurisdiction is the sole responsibility of the purchaser or reader. The Author and Publisher assume no responsibility or liability whatsoever on the behalf of any purchaser or reader of these materials. Any perceived slights of specific people or organizations are unintentional.

As with any business and/or individual, your results may vary, and will be based on your individual capacity, business experience, expertise, and level of desire. There are no guarantees concerning the level of success you may experience. Each individual's success depends on his or her background, dedication, desire and motivation.

The use of this Multimedia Learning Resource should be based on your own due diligence and you agree that our company is not liable for any success or failure of your learning goals that is directly or indirectly related to the purchase and use of this book.

免責事項・著作権

　このマルチメディア学習教材は著者であるボリス・ポルード（Boris　Poludo）が所有権を有しております。個人の使用目的のみが許されます。複製や配布をすることは違法です。この教材のいかなる部分も、著者の書面上の許可なく複製、検索システムに保存、いかなる種類またはいかなる手段（電子通信、機械通信、コピー、録音、翻訳）での伝送、また、これを使って二次創作物を作成する事を行なってはなりません。このマルチメディア学習教材に含まれる情報は全て教育資料を意図としており、効果を保証したり、この本で紹介された学習法、指示、提案を用いる事によって引き起こされた結果に関し、一切の責任を負うものではありません。この教材は、著者と出版者が法的、会計的、またはその他の専門的なアドバイスを提供するものではない事の理解を以って提供されるものとします。もし、法的または専門的な支援が必要とされるならば、優秀な専門家のサービスを求めるべきです。

　私、ボリス・ポルード（Boris　Poludo）は、この教材によって当事者が取った行動によって起こった事に対し、一切の責任を負いません。この出版物に記載される情報については出来る限りの確認が行なわれましたが、著者も発行者も内容についての間違いや脱落、間違った解釈などについては一切責任を負いません。この出版物は、法律や会計に関してのアドバイスとして使用されるものではありません。著者と発行者は、ここに含まれる情報は州または地域の法令によって変わる事がある事を強調致します。使用者は皆、どの州や地域の法令が使用者の事情に当てはまるか、優秀な専門家の助言を求める事を薦められるものとします。この出版物の購入者や読者は、この教材と情報を使用する事の責任を負うものとします。カナダ及び他の全ての地域でビジネスをすることにより当てはまる全ての法律や規則（国、州、地域、政府の専門職資格、商行為、広報など）に則る事は、購入者または読者の責任です。著者と発行者はこの教材の購入者や読者の代わりに責任を取るものではありません。仮に特定の個人や会社にとって侮辱に取れるように感じられる事があったとしてもそれは意図に反する事であります。

　どんなビジネスや個人でも同じですが、使用者の結果は様々であり、個人の能力、ビジネス経験、専門知識や技能、どれだけ達成したいかという熱望の度合いによって変わります。あなたが経験するかも知れない成功の度合いに関して保証は致しません。個々の成功の度合いは、個人の背景、献身や、切望の度合い、そして意欲によって違います。

　このマルチメディア教材の使用の際には、あなた自身の勤勉が基礎にあるべきであり、この教材の購入や使用に直接または間接的に関係するあなたの学習目標の達成の成功や失敗は我が社には関係がない事をあなたは承知するものとします。

Content

目次

About the Author

This book is written by Canadian of Russian origin Boris Poludo. Born and raised in the Russian Far East, Boris always had an incredible nature of exploration and thirst for learning an amazing range of subjects. Trying to adapt to completely unknown, foreign environments, unexplored different sides of life, Boris is drawn to recreational flying and the art of cooking, classical singing, composition and recording, information technology and sailing.

Boris studied aviation but at the age of 27 took on vocal performing arts at the State Academy of Music and rapidly changes his career leaving a good job at the International airport rescue team to join one of the state's most famous music groups as one of the leading tenors.

In 1992 the idea of learning languages and exploring new cultures led Boris to leave Russia for Canada. Absolutely fascinating, spectacular city of Vancouver of Beautiful British Columbia Canada became his home ever since.

An incredible teaching talent developed over the years and combined with restless interest in information systems and psychology resulting in establishing training facility. Boris started teaching advanced concepts and methodology of software quality assurance, quality control and testing.

Over the years of learning and teaching experience, Boris developed ROLL (Read Out Loud and Learn) methodology. This methodology was successfully tested in Software Quality Analysis and Testing training in Vancouver.

Using Boris's ROLL methodology makes learning English much easier when you just starting.

著者紹介

こ の本はロシア出身のカナダ人、ボリス・ポルード(Boris Pludo)によって書か
れました。ロシアの極東に生まれ育ち、ボリスは常に未知を探求したいとい
う気質を持ち、多くの幅広い事柄に対して学ぶ意欲がありました。全く今まで知
らなかった事、未知の環境、まだ足を踏み入れたことがない人生の別の顔を受け
入れようとして、ボリスはレクリエーション目的の飛行活動、クッキング、クラシッ
ク音楽の歌唱、作曲と録音、ITと、セーリングに惹かれていきました。

ボリスは航空学を学びましたが、27歳の時に国立音楽アカデミーの声楽家の仕
事を引き受け、国際空港の救助隊での良い仕事から、国家有数の有名楽団での
主要なテノール歌手の一人へと急速にキャリア変更をしました。

語学を習い、新しい文化を探求するというアイディアが結果として1992年にボ
リスがロシアを去り、カナダへとやってくる事となりました。それ以降は、カナダの
ブリティッシュコロンビア州にある、全く魅惑的で素晴らしいバンクーバー市を住
まいとし、住み続けています。

その素晴らしい教授力は長い年月をかけて培われ、情報システムと心理学に対し
ての止まない興味と組み合わさって、教育施設を設立する結果となりました。ボリ
スは、ソフトウェアの品質保証そして、品質コントロールとテストの先進概念と方
法論を教え始めました。

長年の、学びと教えの経験から、ボリスはROLL(声に出して読んで学ぶ)方法論を
確立しました。この方法論はバンクーバーに於いてのソフトウェア品質分析とテス
トのトレーニングで試験済みです。

ボリスのROLL方法論は英語を学び始めた人にとって、英語を自分のものにし易
くします。

Author's Welcome

Thank you for purchasing my book and welcome to the new world, the world of new culture, new philosophy and new approach to life.

Speaking a foreign language, especially English, opens an incredible amount of opportunities in life, such as career development, improving self-confidence and adapting to completely new social environments. You will find yourself making new friends. You will find that shopping becomes a fun experience instead of constant frustration. Communicating with people at stores and community centers will become much easier. Generally you will find yourself to be a much happier person.

It is very important to remember that no book in the world will ever teach you to speak English. It takes an extraordinary amount of confidence, dedication and consistent effort to pursue your goal to success. Most importantly you have to believe in yourself.

When you complete Day One of this book you will instantly realize how much you can learn in only one lesson. You will be encouraged by your achievement. Make the most of it and try to bring solid consistency to your learning effort. This will make a huge difference in getting where you want to get – start speaking English.

I hope you will find this book to be a great instructional resource in your learning process.

Remember, your success is in your own hands.

著者のご挨拶

私の本をご購入頂き有難うございます。そして、新しい世界にようこそ！新しい文化、新しい哲学、人生への新しいアプローチの世界へ。

外国語を話すこと(特に英語)は、キャリア開発、自分への自信を増やすこと、全く新しい社会環境へ順応すること等、人生に於いては信じられない程多くの機会をもたらします。新しい友達も出来るでしょう。ショッピングが、絶え間ない失望から、楽しい経験に変わっていることに気がつくでしょう。店やコミュニティセンターで人とコミュニケーションを取る事がもっと簡単になるでしょう。大抵は自分自身がずっとハッピーな人間になっていることに気が付く事でしょう。

とても大切な事なので心に留めて頂きたいのは、世界中のどんな本も英語を話すという事を教えてくれる本はなく、今後もないだろうという事です。話すというあなたのゴールを達成させるには、途方もない量の自信と、献身、絶え間ない努力が必要です。最も重要な事は、自分を信じるという事です。

この本の一日目を終えたら、ひとつのレッスンだけで沢山のことが学んで頂けるこがを分かって頂けると思います。ご自分が達成出来た事によって自信がつく事でしょう。出来るだけ有効活用され、学ぶ努力を怠らずしっかりと持ち続けようとして頂きたいと思います。この事が、ご自分の目標とされる所－英語を話し始めること－に行き着くためには大変大きな差をつける秘訣となります。

この本があなたが英語を学ぶ上で、素晴らしい学習法であると分かって頂ける事を望みます。

覚えておいて下さい、成功はあなたの手中にあります。

Brief history

This book is written based on my own experience of learning English in a very short period of time. This chapter is a brief excurse into the origin of technique used in this learning approach.

Moving to Canada at the age of 29, I could not speak any English what so ever. Someone said to me at the time:

> *Oh, just don't worry about anything, living in this country you will start speaking English in one year without doing anything about it!*

I cannot believe how naive should one be to believe that this is true. Never the less I did. Being told this I was not seriously concerned with luck of effort on my side and evidently lost the whole year of my life waiting for miracle to happen.

Do not believe anyone who tells you that you will eventually start speaking English without learning it. It will never happen.

When I realized that nothing was happening and my English was not getting any better, I got extremely frustrated with myself and started to take actions.

I have buried myself in books, tapes, CDs and started studying. Many books came from a local library. Textbooks, different English studying courses, audio materials made my head spinning. It was just too much. I needed a plan and a system.

Making learning English my full time job, I walked out of my little rented room in center town of Ottawa in 30 days speaking English acceptable enough for communication in all aspects of everyday life. Yes you are right - 30 days more than 10. If you don't have a clearly defined system, approach and single resource it might take you much longer than 30 days. It takes some people years to learn and yet they still speak very poor English.

In this book, I am giving you the solid system, well defined and clearly described approach as well as all the text and audio resources with very precise day-to-day instructions on how to proceed and progress with your learning.

簡単な背景・歴史

こ の本は、私自身がとても短い期間で英語を学んだという経験に基づいて書かれています。このチャプターはこの学習方法で使われているテクニックの源への短い小旅行です。

29歳の時にカナダに移り、私は全く英語が話せませんでした。そんな時誰かが私にこう言いました。

> 66 全く心配することないよ、この国に住んでいるのだから全く何もしなくても英語を1年で話し始めるよ。 99

これが本当だなんて信じるには、どれだけ世間知らずでなければならないだろうと、信じられないくらいです。しかし、それにも関わらず私は信じたのです。こう言われて、自分の努力が足りない事を真剣には気にかけず、疑いもなく、人生の丸々1年を、奇跡が起こるのを待ちわびて過ごしたのです。

勉強しなくても、いずれ話し始めるよという人を信じないで下さい。そんな事は絶対に起こりません。

何も起こらず、私の英語が全く良くなっていない事に気づくと、私は自分自身に非常に腹が立って行動を起こし始めました。

本、カセットテープ、CDに埋もれ勉強を始めました。多くの本は地元の図書館からでした。教科書や、色々な英語学習コース、音声教材が私の頭をくらくらさせました。その多さに圧倒されてしまったのです。私には計画とシステムが必要だったのです。

英語を学ぶことをフルタイムの仕事のようにして、結果、30日後には日常生活のどんな場面においてもコミュニケーションが出来る許容範囲には十分なスピーキング力をつけてオタワの中心地にその時借りていた小さな部屋から歩き出したのです。そうです、お気づきの通りです、10日ではなく30日です。もしはっきりしたシステム、方法と、リソースをお持ちでなければ、30日よりずっと長くかかるでしょう。人によっては何年も学んでいてもほとんど英語が話せない人もいます。

この本では、私があなたにしっかりとしたシステムをお渡しします。このシステムは、はっきりと定義され、学習方法の内容が明確に説明されており、また、文章と音声源と、どのように日々勉強を進めていけばいいかとても詳細な指示が入っています。

13

Who should Read This Book

This book is intended for those who would like to learn how to speak Basic English in a very short period of time.

If you would like to have fun learning English then this book is for you.

If you would like to make new friends then this book is for you.

If you are planning to travel to an English speaking country then this book is for you.

If you would like to be able to speak to others to discuss sports or politics then this book is for you.

If you are afraid to pick up the phone in your hotel room or at home because you think your will not understand the caller then this book is for you.

If you think that your English is not good enough to find work then this book is for you.

If you think that your English is not good enough to move on with your life by finding better paying job then this book is for you.

If you need to pick up some English very quick to start with your new job then this book is for you.

If you think that your confidence level suffers because you don't speak and understand English then this book is for you.

If you need to be able to better express yourself in English then this book is for you.

If you believe that your overall well-being can be improved if you spoke English then this book is for you.

If you are bored and don't know what to do that would be fun and really useful then this book is for you.

If you would like to better understand news on the radio, newspapers or TV then this book is for you.

If you are planning to learn English seriously and don't know where to start then this book is for you.

誰がこの本を読むべきか

こ の本はベーシックな英語をとても短い期間で話せるようになる方法を学びたい方を対象としています。

もし英語を学ぶことを楽しみたいのであれば、この本はあなたに向いています。

もし新しい友達を作りたいのであれば、この本はあなたに向いています。

もし英語が話されている国へ旅行しようと計画を立てているのであれば、この本はあな たに向いています。

もしあなたがスポーツや政治について人と意見を交わし合いたいのであれば、この本はあなたに向いています。

もしホテルの部屋や自宅で、相手の言っている事が分からないと思うために電話を取る事が怖ければ、この本はあなたに向いています。

もしあなたがあなたの英語が仕事を得るには十分でないと思うならば、この本はあなたに向いています。

もしあなたがより良いお給料の仕事を見つけて、人生を変えたいならば、この本はあなたに向いています。

もしあなたが、新しく決まった仕事のために、早く多少の英語を覚えなくてはいけないのであれば、この本はあなたに向いています。

もしあなたが英語が話せない、分からないという理由で自信がなくなってきているのであれば、この本はあなたに向いています。

もしあなたが英語で自分自身をより上手く表現しないといけないのであれば、この本はあなたに向いています。

もしあなたの心身的身体的幸福度が英語を話せるという事によって上がると信じるのであれば、この本はあなたに向いています。

もしあなたが退屈していて、何をしたら楽しくそして役に立つのか分からなければ、この本はあなたに向いています。

もしあなたが、ラジオや新聞そしてテレビの内容をより良く理解したいのであれば、この本はあなたに向いています。

もしあなたが真剣に英語を学びたいと思っているのだけど、どこから始めたら良いか分 からないのであれば、この本はあなたに向いています。

Learning Approach

In this book I have incorporated 100 most commonly used English words equally distributed between all ten lessons for ease of use.

Here also I am presenting my new ROLL methodology of learning a new foreign language.

ROLL stands for Read Out Loud and Learn

It is indeed very simple concept of approaching learning process with the emphasis on reading the content of each Day out loud. I will be repeating instructions and the importance of following it at the beginning of each lesson.

Each Day is broken down into 4 parts.

1. Vocabulary.	10 new English words to memorize
2. Topic.	Text for reading exercise
3. Dialogue.	Conversation of two people for reading exercise
4. Exercise.	Practice exercise examples.

The process of learning any language can be broken down into five stages. I refer to it as learning lifecycle.

1. See

First step in learning a term, phrase of sentence is visual perception. Once you see the term or a phrase you will be able to recognize it next time you see it in different context.

2. Read out loud

It is extremely important to read all the contents out loud. Being able to pronounce the term, phrase of sentence is not less important than understanding it. You should not be concerned with pronunciation in terms of accent, which you will always have to certain extent but more with confidence that you are speaking with.

学習方法

こ の本では、私はよく使われる英単語を100語、使い易いように10日間のレッスンの中に均等に組み込みました。

ここで、わたしはまた、自身の新しいROLLという外国語を学ぶ方法論を提示しています。

ROLLは、Read Out Loud(声に出して読み) and Learn (学ぶ)の、それぞれ頭文字を取ったものです。

これは、本当にシンプルな学習コンセプトで、それぞれの日の内容を声に出して読む事に重点が置かれています。それぞれのレッスンの最初に、やり方とROLLメソッドを行なう重要性が繰り返し書いてあります。

それぞれの日は4つのパートに分かれます。

1. ボキャブラリー　　覚えるべき10の新しい英単語
2. トピック　　　　　音読練習の為の文章
3. ダイアローグ　　　音読練習の為の二人の登場人物の会話
4. エクササイズ　　　練習問題

どんな言語を学ぶプロセスも5つの段階に分けられます。これを私は学習のライフサイクルと呼びます。

1. 見る

用語やフレーズ、文を学ぶ最初のステップは視覚からです。　一度、用語やフレーズを見ると、次回別の内容で見るた時に、「ああ、前に見たことがある」と気がつくことができます。

2. 声に出して読む

全ての内容を声に出して読むことは非常に大切な事です。用語やフレーズ、文を発音出来ることはそれらの内容を理解する事に比べて重要度が低いといった事はありません。ただ、アクセントに関しては、ある程度はどうしてもあるものなので、それ程気にする必要はありません、それよりは、スピーキングに自信が持てるようにする事を気にかけてください。

17

3. Hear

Listening to the topic you are studying gives you the opportunity to train your second language hearing perception, as well as the chance for pronunciation comparison exercise. Listen to the audio part of the topic, then read the topic out loud comparing your pronunciation with the way it is pronounced on the tape.

4. Memorize

Progressing Day by Day you will find yourself memorizing new words, phrases and even sentences. You may think that you may only memorize a small fraction of what you learned but in fact you will remember and understand all of it without even realizing it. As you move further with your learning, the more you will realize that you understand TV and radio programs better and some terms and phrases you will even be surprised as to where you might know them from. Try to memorize as much as you can.

5. Use

This is what the whole thing is all about. Being able to use what you learn, right? Try to do everything possible to put yourself in the position where you will have no choice but to speak English. Here it is extremely important to understand this: Do not concentrate on your pronunciation or on grammar. Remember the goal is to start speaking and understand but concentrating on your mistakes too much at the very beginning may slow down your learning tremendously. So SPEAK AWAY .

Once you use a term or a phrase in a sentence while talking to someone you may consider that this term or phrase is now in your active vocabulary.

You would be surprised how many people have an extremely rich vocabulary and extensive knowledge of grammar but still don't speak English very well. The lack of practice or an opportunity to communicate with an English-speaking person is the most common reason.

How to use this multimedia learning resource

Remember that the most important concept of this entire book is –
READING OUT LOUD.

3. 聞く

自分が勉強しているトピックを聞く事は、あなたの学んでいる言語を聞く力を育てる機会であり、また、発音の比較の訓練にもなります。トピックの音声部分を聞いて、それからトピックを、自分の発音とテープの発音を比べながら、声に出して読んで下さい。

4. 覚える

一日一日進みながら、ご自分が新しい単語、フレーズや文を覚えていることに気がつくでしょう。勉強したことの内、少ししか覚えていないように感じるかも知れませんが、実際には自分で気がつかなくても、勉強したことの全てを覚えて理解しているでしょう。学習が進むにつれて、テレビやラジオ番組がより理解出来る様になっていることに気がつき、また、何処で聞いて知っているのか分からない言い回しやフレーズが理解出来る様になっていることに気がつくでしょう。本書で学習する内容を出来る限り覚えてください。

5. 使う

全てはこれに尽きます。学んだ事を使えるようになる事ですね。自分を、英語を使うしかない状況に出来る限り置いて下さい。その中で、以下の事を理解する事がとても大切です－発音や文法に固執しないで下さい。目標は英語を話し始め理解することであり、学び始めに自身の間違いに集中しすぎる事は、あなたの学習速度をとてつもなく遅くします。ですので、沢山話してください。

一度言い回しやフレーズを文中で、誰かに話しかけるのに使ったなら、それらはあなたが使いこなせる表現になったと思っていいです。

どれだけの人が、非常に沢山の語彙を持っていて文法についてよく知っていても、まだ英語を上手に話せないかあなたは驚くことでしょう。練習不足や、英語を話す人とのコミュニケーションの機会が無い事が一番よくある原因です。

このマルチメディア学習法の使い方

この本全体の最も重要なコンセプトは何か忘れないで下さい－**声に出して読むということです。**

ROLL methodology is what will get you where you need to get really fast.

Remember - this is very, if not the most important exercise in this book. Read out loud the entire text first until your reading becomes flawless. By flawless I mean that you don't need to pause to read the next word or sentence.

You absolutely must read the text **as many times as it takes** to achieve the flawless reading.

Once the flawless reading is achieved, listen to the topic audio with attention to pronunciation details. Now read the text out loud again and compare the pronunciation with the Day audio.

1. *Review the Day*, content covering all 4 parts of the Day.

2. *New Vocabulary* - Start with each Day by reading each new word in New Vocabulary part of the Day and find its meaning in the mirror translation page.

3. *Topic* - Read through the topic part of the Day. Make sure you are reading out loud.

4. Understand the topic content by reading a mirror translation page.

5. If you can record yourself reading do so. Make a note in the text where you think you need to make your reading better, and try to read the text again until satisfied.

6. *Dialogue* – Follow the exact same approach to work your way through dialogue as you used for Topic. Read and review the mirror translation page for better understanding, then work on reading the dialogue out loud until you read the entire dialogue with ease.

7. *Exercise* – follow the instruction and complete each Day exercise part.

ROLLメソッドは、あなたがとても早く到達したい所に到達させてくれます。

忘れないで下さい―もしこの本の中で一番大切な練習ではないとしたとしても、これはとても大切な事です。最初に、本文全てをあなたの音読が完璧になるまで、声に出して読んで下さい。完璧とは、あなたが新しい単語や文を読むのに止まったりする必要がなく読めるという事です。

完璧に読めるようになるまで絶対に何度も本文を読まなくてはなりません。

完璧に読めるようになったら、トピック本文を音声で聞くのですが、その際に発音に注意して聞いてください。それからトピック本文をまた声に出して読み、自分の発音を音声と比べます。

　　1. **その日の復習をする**―その日の内容4パートを全てすること。

　　2. **新しいボキャブラリー**―その日の新しいボキャブラリー部分の一つ一つの新しい単語を読む事から始め、その意味を日本語のページの同じ部分を見て確認します。

　　3. **トピック**―その日のトピックの部分を読みます。声を出して読んで下さい。

　　4. トピックの内容を、日本語のページを読んで理解する。

　　5. もし音読しながらそれを録音できるのであればしてください。読んでいて練習が必要なところに印をつけてください、そして、本文を満足するまで読むようにして下さい。

　　6. **ダイアローグ**―トピックの際にしたのと全く同じ方法を取ってください。より良く理解するために、日本語で書かれた同じページを読んで見直してください、それから声に出して読み簡単に読めるようになるまで続けます。

　　7. **エクササイズ**―指示に従ってそれぞれの日のエクササイズ部分を終えてください。

Day 1

Day one is the exception of the rule and does not consist of four parts as all the other Days. In this Day, you are presented things like Alphabet, Numbers, Calendar, time and the very basics of time construction. Complete this Day without concentrating on memorizing its content. It will come with time.

Alphabet

Using Day 1 audio file listen to how each letter of the alphabet is pronounced and repeat out loud when the audio pauses between each letter of the alphabet.

A a	B b	C c	D d	E e
F f	G g	H h	I i	J j
K k	L l	M m	N n	O o
P p	Q q	R r	S s	T t
U u	V v	W w	X x	Y y
Z z				

1日目

他の全ての日は、1日分がそれぞれ4つのパートから成り立っているのですが、1日目にはそのルールが当てはまりません。1日目では、アルファベットや数、カレンダー、時間など、とてもベーシックな時間の表示方法を学びます。内容の暗記に集中しないでこの日を完了してください。時間が経てば自然と覚えられます。

アルファベット

1日目の音声ファイルを使って、それぞれのアルファベットの文字がどのように発音されているのか注意深く聞き、アルファベットの文字の音声の切れ間で、声に出してリピートして下さい。

A a	B b	C c	D d	E e
F f	G g	H h	I i	J j
K k	L l	M m	N n	O o
P p	Q q	R r	S s	T t
U u	V v	W w	X x	Y y
Z z				

Day
1

Numbers

Listen how each Number is pronounced and repeat out loud when audio pauses between numbers. Don't try to memorize all these numbers the very first time. Instead do it repeatedly time after time. You may do it without even thinking about memorizing it and do it mechanically. Just do it as many time as you can, until it makes you sick. It does work really well.

1 One	2 Two	3 Three	4 Four	5 Five
6 Six	7 Seven	8 Eight	9 Nine	10 Ten

11 Eleven	12 Twelve	13 Thirteen	14 Fourteen	15 Fifteen
16 Sixteen	17 Seventeen	18 Eighteen	19 Nineteen	20 Twenty

21 Twenty one	22 Twenty two	23 Twenty three	24 Twenty four	25 Twenty five
26 Twenty six	27 Twenty seven	28 Twenty eight	29 Twenty nine	30 Thirty

40 Forty	50 Fifty	60 Sixty	70 Seventy	80 Eighty
90 Ninety	100 One hundred			

数字

それぞれの数字がどの様に発音されているかよく聞いて、音声が途切れる合間に声に出してリピートして下さい。これらの数全てを始めて1回で全て覚えようとはしないで下さい。そうではなく、その後も何度も繰り返してください。覚えようとしてやるのではなく、機械的にやっていいです。もういやだなと思うくらいまで、何度も何度も出来る限り繰り返して下さい。この方法が本当に良く効きます。

1 一	2 二	3 三	4 四	5 五
6 六	7 七	8 八	9 九	10 十

11 十一	12 十二	13 十三	14 十四	15 十五
16 十六	17 十七	18 十八	19 十九	20 二十

21 二十一	22 二十二	23 二十三	24 二十四	25 二十五
26 二十六	27 二十七	28 二十八	29 二十九	30 三十

40 四十	50 五十	60 六十	70 七十	80 八十
90 九十	100 百			

25

Day 1 Calendar

Listen how each day of the week is pronounced and repeat out loud when audio pauses.

Monday	Tuesday	Wednesday	Thursday	Friday
Saturday	Sunday			

Listen how each month of the year is pronounced and repeat out loud when audio pauses.

January	February	March	April
May	June	July	August
September	October	November	December

カレンダー

それぞれの曜日がどのように発音されているか注意深く聞き、音声の切れ間で声に出してリピートして下さい。

月曜日	火曜日	水曜日	木曜日	金曜日
土曜日	日曜日			

それぞれの月の名前がどのように発音されているか注意深く聞き、音声の切れ間で声に出してリピートして下さい。

一月	二月	三月	四月
五月	六月	七月	八月
九月	十月	十一月	十二月

Time

North American 24-hour clock time is measured in two segments AM and PM.

Everything between midnight and noon is referred to as AM hours and between noon and midnight as PM.

12:00 AM	Midnight
12:00 PM	Noon
5:00 AM	5 o'clock in the morning
5:00 PM	5 o'clock in the afternoon

There are several ways to say time. It depends on whether it is the first or second half of the hour.

5:20	- Five twenty - Twenty past five - Twenty after five
5:30	- Five thirty - Half past five - Thirty to six
5:40	- Five forty - Twenty to six

時間

一日日

北米の２４時間は、午前（AM）と午後(PM)の２つの区切りにて表されます。

夜中の１２時から昼の１２時までの間が午前（AM）と呼ばれ、昼の１２時から夜中の１２時までの間が午後(PM)と呼ばれます。

12:00 AM	午前零時(夜中の０時、夜中の１２時)
12:00 PM	正午(お昼の１２時)
5:00 AM	朝５時（ちょうど）
5:00 PM	午後５時（ちょうど）

時間の表し方には幾つかの言い方があります。それは、その時間が１時間の最初の半分なのか残りの半分なのかによります。

5:20	-5時２０分 -5時を２０分過ぎたところ -5時の２０分後
5:30	-5時３０分 -5時から３０分(１時間の半分)過ぎたところ -6時になるまであと３０分
5:40	-5時４０分 -6時の２０分前

Greetings

Listen how each greeting is pronounced and repeat out loud when audio pauses between greetings.

Saying Hello

Hi

Hello

Good morning

Good afternoon

Good evening

Good night
(normally used before bed time)

How are you

How are you doing

What's up

Saying Good bye

Good Bye

Bye

Bye bye

Have a good day

Enjoy your day

See you later

Talk to you later

Later

See ya

挨拶

それぞれの挨拶がどのように発音されているか注意深く聞き、挨拶の合間で音声が切れる際に、声に出してリピートして下さい。

会った時の挨拶

こんにちは (カジュアル)

こんにちは (いつでも使える)

おはようございます

こんにちは (午後の挨拶)

こんばんは

おやすみなさい (通常床につく前)

お元気ですか

如何お過ごしですか

何か起きている？

別れる時の挨拶

さようなら

バーイ

バイバイ

良い一日を

(一日を)楽しんでね

また後でね

また後でお話しましょう

後でね

じゃあね

Past, present and future time construction

Expressing time in English is far more complex than just defining Past, Present and Future in a sentence, but at this point you do not need to be concerned with anything else other than what is given to you in this Book. Remember the goal you are trying to achieve is to start speaking English in very short period of time, your short-term goal – understand others and confidently explain yourself.

Listen to the audio multiple times. It is recommended that you listen to it when you are doing something else other than learning English. Have it on while doing something around the house. Try to have it on as much as you can. You may even think about something else other than learning, but it still does the trick. You will still accumulate both, the pronunciation techniques as well as vocabulary in terms of usage within the phrases and sentences.

Read the contents of all three Present, Past and Future tables. You should read the entire contents regardless of the similarity and find places where you experience difficulties, then read only those sentences or phrases until your reading becomes flawless. Remember you can never have enough of reading. All of the reading that you will have to do in this book should only be done OUT LOUD. The ROLL methodology (read out loud and learn) will be presented in Day 2.

Once you have perfected difficult places, repeat reading the entire contents again.

Make sure to do all the reading out loud. I cannot stress enough the importance of reading out loud.

Just reading quietly and moving your eyes along the lines of text will not make much difference if at all.

過去・現在・未来時制の構造

英語で時を表現することは単に過去、現在、未来を文中で定義するよりも遥かに複雑です、しかしこの時点ではこの本で提供されていること以外を気にする必要はありません。あなたが達成しようとしているゴールはとても短い期間で英語を話し始める事であり、あなたの目下の目標は、相手の言っていることを理解し、自信を持ってあなた自身のことをお話しすることです。

音声を何度か聞いて下さい。英語を勉強している時ではなく、何か別のことをしているときに聞くのをお勧めします。家の中で何かしている時に音声をかけてください。
出来るだけ何度もかけるようにして下さい。かけている間、勉強ではなく何か別の事を考えるかもしれませんが、それでも効果があるのです。フレーズや文で使われている発音やボキャブラリーのどちらも頭に残っていきます。

現在、過去、未来の3つの表にある内容を読んでください。内容が似通っている事に関わらず全ての内容を読んで、そして、難しいと感じる部分を見つけたら、その文章やフレーズだけを完璧に読める様になるまで何度も繰り返して下さい。何度読んでも読み過ぎという事はないという事を覚えておいて下さい。この本を使って読むのは全て、声に出して行なわれなければなりません。このROLL方法論（声に出して読んで学ぶ）は、2日目で提示されます。

難しい部分を克服したら、全体をまた何度も読み返して下さい。

必ず、読む時には声に出して読んで下さい。声に出して読むことの重要性は何度強調しても強調しきれない程です。

精読して、目を文に沿って動かすだけでは全く上達しないという事はないとしても、あまり上達は望めません。

Day 1

Present

Listen how to each sentence is pronounced and repeat out loud when audio pauses between sentences.

I	I am a student. I am learning English. I learn languages. I am a pilot. I am flying an airplane. I fly small airplanes. I am a teacher. I am teaching history. I teach university students. I am a bus driver. I am driving a bus right now. I drive a new bus. I am an engineer. I am working in a construction site. I work long hours.
You	You are a student. You are learning English. You learn languages. You are a pilot. You are flying an airplane. You fly small airplanes. You are a teacher. You are teaching history. You teach university students. You are a bus driver. You are driving a bus right now. You drive a new bus. You are an engineer. You are working on a construction site. You work long hours.
He	He is a student. He is learning English. He learns languages. He is a pilot. He is flying an airplane. He flies small airplanes. He is a teacher. He is teaching history. He teaches university students. He is a bus driver. He is driving bus right now. He drives a new bus. He is an engineer. He is working in a construction site. He works long hours.
She	She is a student. She is learning English. She learns languages. She is a pilot. She is flying an airplane. She flies small airplanes. She is a teacher. She is teaching history. She teaches university students. She is a bus driver. She is driving bus right now. She drives a new bus. She is an engineer. She is working on a construction site. She works long hours.
They	They are students. They are learning English. They learn languages. They are pilots. They are flying airplanes. They fly small airplanes. They are teachers. They are teaching history. They Teach university students. They are bus drivers. They are driving buses in right now. They drive new buses. They are engineers. They are working on a construction site. They work long hours.

現在

それぞれの文がどのように発音されているか注意深く聞き、文の合間で音声が切れる際に、声に出してリピートして下さい。

私は	私は学生です。私は英語を学んでいます。私は言語を学びます。 私はパイロットです。私は飛行機を操縦しています。私は小さな飛行機を操縦します。 私は先生です。私は歴史を教えています。私は大学生を教えます。 私はバスの運転手です。私は今バスを運転中です。私は新しいバスを運転します。 私はエンジニアです。私は建設現場で働いています。私は長時間働きます。
あなたは	あなたは学生です。あなたは英語を学んでいます。あなたは言語を学びます。 あなたはパイロットです。あなたは飛行機を操縦しています。あなたは小さな飛行機を操縦します。 あなたは先生です。あなたは歴史を教えています。あなたは大学生を教えています。 あなたはバスの運転手です。あなたは今バスを運転中です。あなたは新しいバスを運転します。 あなたはエンジニアです。あなたは建設現場で働いています。あなたは長時間働きます。
彼は	彼は学生です。彼は英語を学んでいます。彼は言語を学びます。 彼はパイロットです。彼は飛行機を操縦しています。彼は小さな飛行機を操縦します。 彼は先生です。彼は歴史を教えています。彼は大学生を教えています。 彼はバスの運転手です。彼は今バスを運転中です。彼は新しいバスを運転します。 彼はエンジニアです。彼は建設現場で働いています。彼は長時間働きます。
彼女は	彼女は学生です。彼女は英語を学んでいます。彼女は言語を学びます。 彼女はパイロットです。彼女は飛行機を操縦しています。彼女は小さな飛行機を操縦します。 彼女は先生です。彼女は歴史を教えています。彼女は大学生を教えます。 彼女はバスの運転手です。彼女は今バスを運転中です。彼女は新しいバスを運転します。 彼女はエンジニアです。彼女は建設現場で働いています。彼女は長時間働きます。
彼らは	彼らは学生です。彼らは英語を学んでいます。彼らは言語を学びます。 彼らはパイロットです。彼らは飛行機を操縦しています。彼らは小さな飛行機を操縦します。 彼らは先生です。彼らは歴史を教えています。彼らは大学生を教えます。 彼らはバスの運転手です。彼らは今バスを運転中です。彼らは新しいバスを運転します。 彼らはエンジニアです。彼らは建設現場で働いています。彼らは長時間働きます。

Past

I	I was a student. I was learning English. I learned languages. I was a pilot. I was flying an airplane. I flew small airplanes. I was a teacher. I was teaching history. I taught university students. I was a bus driver. I was driving a bus in the morning. I drove a new bus. I was an engineer. I was working on a construction site. I worked long hours.
You	You were a student. You were learning English. You learn languages. You were a pilot. You were flying an airplane. You flew small airplanes. You were a teacher. You were teaching history. You taught university students. You were a bus driver. You were driving a bus in the morning. You drove a new bus. You were an engineer. You were working on a construction site. You worked long hours.
He	He was a student. He was learning English. He learned languages. He was a pilot. He was flying an airplane. He flied small airplanes. He was a teacher. He was teaching history. He taught university students. He was a bus driver. He was driving a bus in the morning. He drove a new bus. He was an engineer. He was working on a construction site. He worked long hours.
She	She was a student. She was learning English. She learned languages. She was a pilot. She was flying an airplane. She flew small airplanes. She was a teacher. She was teaching history. She taught university students. She was a bus driver. She was driving a bus in the morning. She drove a new bus. She was an engineer. He was working on a construction site. She worked long hours.
They	They were a student. They were learning English. They learn languages. They were pilots. They were flying airplanes. They flew small airplanes. They were a teacher. They were teaching history last year. They taught university students. They were bus drivers. They were driving buses in the morning. They drov new buses. They were engineers. They were working on a construction site. They worked long hours.

過去

私は	私は学生でした。私は英語を学んでいました。私は言語を学びました。 私はパイロットでした。私は飛行機を操縦していました。私は小さな飛行機を操縦しました。 私は先生でした。私は歴史を教えていました。私は大学生を教えました。 私はバスの運転手でした。私は朝、バスを運転していました。私は新しいバスを運転しました。 私はエンジニアでした。私は建設現場で働いていました。私は長時間働きました。
あなたは	あなたは学生でした。あなたは英語を学んでいました。あなたは言語を学びました。 あなたはパイロットでした。あなたは飛行機を操縦していました。あなたは小さな飛行機を操縦しました。 あなたは先生でした。あなたは歴史を教えていました。あなたは大学生を教えました。 あなたはバスの運転手でした。あなたは朝、バスを運転していました。あなたは新しいバスを運転しました。 あなたはエンジニアでした。あなたは建設現場で働いていました。あなたは長時間働きました。
彼は	彼は学生でした。彼は英語を学んでいました。彼は言語を学びました。 彼はパイロットでした。彼は飛行機を操縦していました。彼は小さな飛行機を操縦しました。 彼は先生でした。彼は歴史を教えていました。彼は大学生を教えました。 彼はバスの運転手でした。彼は朝、バスを運転していました。彼は新しいバスを運転しました。 彼はエンジニアでした。彼は建設現場で働いていました。彼は長時間働きました。
彼女は	彼女は学生でした。彼女は英語を学んでいました。彼女は言語を学びました。 彼女はパイロットでした。彼女は飛行機を操縦していました。彼女は小さな飛行機を操縦しました。 彼女は先生でした。彼女は歴史を教えていました。彼女は大学生を教えました。 彼女はバスの運転手でした。彼女は朝、バスを運転していました。彼女は新しいバスを運転しました。 彼女はエンジニアでした。彼女は建設現場で働いていました。彼女は長時間働きました。
彼らは	彼らは学生でした。彼らは英語を学んでいました。彼らは言語を学びました。 彼らはパイロットでした。彼らは飛行機を操縦していました。彼らは小さな飛行機を操縦しました。 彼らは先生でした。彼らは去年歴史を教えていました。彼らは大学生を教えました。 彼らはバスの運転手でした。彼らは朝、バスを運転していました。彼らは新しいバスを運転しました。 彼らはエンジニアでした。彼らは建設現場で働いていました。彼らは長時間働きました。

Future

Day 1		

I	I will be a student. I will be learning English. I will learn languages. I will be a pilot. I will be flying an airplane. I will fly small airplanes. I will be a teacher. I will be teaching history. I will teach university students. I will be a bus driver. I will be driving city buses. I will drive a new bus. I will be an engineer. I will be working on a construction site. I will work long hours.
You	You will be a student. You will be learning English. You will learn languages. You will be a pilot. You will be flying an airplane. You will fly small airplanes. You will be a teacher. You will be teaching history. You will teach university students. You will be a bus driver. You will be driving a city bus. You will drive a new bus. You will be an engineer. You will be working on a construction site. You will work long hours.
He	He will be a student. He will be learning English. He will learns languages. He will be a pilot. He will be flying an airplane. He will fly small airplanes. He will be a teacher. He will be teaching history. He will teach university students. He will be a bus driver. He will be driving city bus. He will drive a new bus. He will be an engineer. He will be working on a construction site. He will work long hours.
She	She will be a student. She will be learning English. She will learn languages. She will be a pilot. She will be flying an airplane. She will fly small airplanes. She will be a teacher. She will be teaching history. She will teach university students. She will be a bus driver. She will be driving a city bus. She will drives a new bus. She will be an engineer. She will be working on a construction site. She will work long hours.
They	They will be students. They will be learning English. They will learn languages. They will be pilots. They will be flying airplanes. They will fly small airplanes. They will be teachers. They will be teaching history. They will teach university students. They will be bus drivers. They will be driving city buses. They drive new buses. They will be engineers. They will be working on a construction site. They will work long hours.

未来

私は	私は学生になるでしょう。私は英語を学んでいるでしょう。私は言語を学ぶでしょう。 私はパイロットになるでしょう。私は飛行機を操縦しているでしょう。私は小さい飛行機を操縦するでしょう。 私は先生になるでしょう。私は歴史を教えているでしょう。私は大学生を教えるでしょう。 私はバスの運転手になるでしょう。私は市バスを運転していることでしょう。私は新しいバスを運転するでしょう。 私はエンジニアになるでしょう。私は建設現場で働いていることでしょう。私は長時間働くでしょう。
あなたは	あなたは学生になるでしょう。あなたは英語を学んでいるでしょう。あなたは言語を学ぶでしょう。 あなたはパイロットになるでしょう。あなたは飛行機を操縦しているでしょう。あなたは小さい飛行機を操縦するでしょう。 あなたは先生になるでしょう。あなたは歴史を教えているでしょう。あなたは大学生を教えるでしょう。 あなたはバスの運転手になるでしょう。あなたは市バスを運転していることでしょう。あなたは新しいバスを運転するでしょう。 あなたはエンジニアになるでしょう。あなたは建設現場で働いていることでしょう。あなたは長時間働くでしょう。
彼は	彼は学生になるでしょう。彼は英語を学んでいるでしょう。彼は言語を学ぶでしょう。 彼はパイロットになるでしょう。彼は飛行機を操縦しているでしょう。彼は小さい飛行機を操縦するでしょう。 彼は先生になるでしょう。彼は歴史を教えているでしょう。彼は大学生を教えるでしょう。 彼はバスの運転手になるでしょう。彼は市バスを運転していることでしょう。彼は新しいバスを運転するでしょう。 彼はエンジニアになるでしょう。彼は建設現場で働いていることでしょう。彼は長時間働くでしょう。
彼女は	彼女は学生になるでしょう。彼女は英語を学んでいるでしょう。彼女は言語を学ぶでしょう。 彼女はパイロットになるでしょう。彼女は飛行機を操縦しているでしょう。彼女は小さい飛行機を操縦するでしょう。 彼女は先生になるでしょう。彼女は歴史を教えているでしょう。彼女は大学生を教えるでしょう。 彼女はバスの運転手になるでしょう。彼女は市バスを運転していることでしょう。彼女は新しいバスを運転するでしょう。 彼女はエンジニアになるでしょう。彼女は建設現場で働いているでしょう。彼女は長時間働くでしょう。
彼らは	彼らは学生になるでしょう。彼らは英語を学んでいるでしょう。彼らは言語を学ぶでしょう。 彼らはパイロットになるでしょう。彼らは飛行機を操縦しているでしょう。彼らは小さい飛行機を操縦するでしょう。 彼らは先生になるでしょう。彼らは歴史を教えているでしょう。彼らは大学生を教えるでしょう。 彼らはバスの運転手になるでしょう。彼らは市バスを運転している事でしょう。彼らは新しいバスを運転するでしょう。 彼らはエンジニアになるでしょう。彼らは建設現場で働いているでしょう。彼らは長時間働くでしょう。

Day 2

1. Vocabulary

Review meaning of each word in mirror translation page. At this point do not be concerned if you don't completely understand the meaning of each one of the words.

Listen to the Day 2 audio file and read out loud each word in the Vocabulary section repeating each word after the narrator.

Repeat the process until you are satisfied with your reading and pronunciation.

The
Be
To
Of
And
A
In
That
Have
I

2. Topic

Working with your topics is no different than working with your dialogues or exercises.

First read through the text to gain some understanding of it by working with the mirror translation page. Don't hesitate to make marks right in the book with a pencil if you need to.

Read the entire text Out Loud as many times as it takes you to achieve flawless reading. You have to get to the stage where your reading gets easy and you don't have to pause between words and phrases.

Listen to the audio provided with this lesson and compare your pronunciation with how it is pronounced by the narrator.

二日目

1. ボキャブラリー

日本語で書かれてある方のページ(本ページ)をご覧になりそれぞれの単語の意味を確認してください。現時点では、単語の意味が完璧に分からなくても心配しないで下さい。

2日目の音声ファイルを聞いて、ボキャブラリーの部分にあるそれぞれの単語をナレーターについて声に出してリピートして下さい。

この作業を自分の音読と発音に満足するまで続けて下さい。

The (特定を表すThe,「その」などと訳せる)

Be (be動詞、いる、ある等)

To (〜に)

Of (〜の)

And (〜と)

A (ひとつの、特定を表さない冠詞で「ある」などと訳せる)

In (〜の中)

That (あれ、あの)

Have (持っている)

I (私は)

2. トピック

トピックを学習することは、ダイアローグやエクササイズを学習するのと変わりません。

最初は対応する日本語の部分と共に英語の本文を読んで、ある程度内容を理解しながら文章の最後まで読み終えます。必要であれば鉛筆などで書き込みを加えて下さい。

文章全てを声に出して読み、スラスラと読める様になるまで、何度も読み返して下さい。単語やフレーズの途中で止まったりする事がなく簡単に読める様になるようになる事が大切です 。

このレッスンの音声を聞いて、ご自分の発音をナレーターの発音と比べて下さい。

Remember that reading the same text out loud over and over again works miracles. You have to read out loud the same text many times until it gets easy. You don't even have to put your brains to work here, just do mechanical reading of the same thing over and over again. Just trust me on this for now and you will be pleasantly surprised how great it works.

My name is Mason. I am an English teacher at Beijing foreign studies university, in Beijing. We have a large ESL program. Our students are from 46 different countries, and they speak 55 different languages.

My students like to ask me questions. Where are you from? Are you married? How old are you? I am from the United States. I was born in Phoenix, but I live in Beijing now. I am married, and I have two daughters. One is in high school, and one is in college. My wife is from the US too. She is a journalist. Don't ask her age! She always says she is 25.

People in My Family

I am Adam. I am 21 years old. I am a student at Columbia University in the City of New York. I study to be an accountant.

My father is 46 years old. He is an architect. He and my mother are divorced. His new wife's name is Jennifer. They have a baby daughter – her name is Linda and she is beautiful!

I have an older sister, Jessica. She is 26. She has long black hair and black eyes. She is medium height and very slim. Jessica is a nurse. She is married. Her husband's name is Tom, he is from Seattle. He is my brother-in-law. Jessica and Tom have a daughter, Jenny. Jenny is five years old. She is my niece, and I am her uncle.

My brother, John, is 28. He is fair-haired, tall and heavyset. He has a mustache and a beard. He is a sales manager. He is a very cheerful guy, and he has a lot of friends. John is married. His wife's name is Anna. She is my sister-in-law. John and Anna have a son. His name Jacob, and he is 3 years old. He is my nephew.

I also have a cousin, Sophia. She lives in Los Angeles. She is 20 years old. She has dark hair and a wonderful smile. She is a student at the University of Southern California. She is single, but she has a boyfriend. His name is Jonathan. He is a professional artist.

My grandmother is about 70 years old. Her name is Emma. She is retired. She has two children and three grandchildren. She lives with her older daughter Isabella in Houston. I visit her every month

何度も何度も同じ文章を読むことが驚くべき効果があることを覚えておいて下さい。同じ文章を何度も何度も、簡単に感じるようになるまで声に出して読まなくてはいけません。頭を使う事は全く必要ないので、機械的に何度も何度も同じ文章を声に出して読んでください。こうする事が大変効果があるという事は、信じ難いかもしれませんが、私を信じてください。続ければきっとこの驚くべき効果を感じて、喜んで頂ける事でしょう。

私の名前はメイソン(Mason)です。私は北京外国語大学の教授です。私達は大きなESL（英語を第二言語として学ぶ）プログラムを持っています。学生達は46カ国出身で、55の言語を話します。

学生達は私に質問をするのが好きです。何処出身ですか？結婚しているのですか？何歳ですか？私はアメリカ出身です。私はフィニックスで生まれましたが、現在は北京に住んでいます。私は結婚していて、二人の娘がいます。一人は高校生で、もう一人はカレッジに通っています。私の妻もアメリカ出身です。妻は記者です。妻の歳は聞かないでください！「25歳です」と、いつも妻は言っています。

私の家族

私はアダム(Adam)です。私は21歳です。私はニューヨーク市にあるコロンビア大学の生徒です。私は会計士になるために勉強しています。

私の父は46歳です。彼は建築家です。父と母は離婚しました。父の新しい奥さんの名前はジェニファー(Jennifer)です。彼らには女の子の赤ちゃんがいます－その子の名前はリンダ(Linda)で、とっても可愛いんです。

私にはジェシカ(Jessica)という姉がいます。26歳です。長い黒髪で、黒い目をしています。背は中くらいで、とてもスリムです。ジェシカは看護師です。結婚しています。彼女の旦那さんはトム(Tom)で、シアトル出身です。彼は義理の兄にあたります。ジェシカとトムには娘がいて、ジェニー(Jenny)といいます。ジェニーは5歳です。ジェシカは私の姪で、ジェシカから見て私は叔父さんです。

私の兄のジョン(John)は28歳です。彼の髪は金髪で、背が高くがっしりしています。口ひげと顎ひげがあります。セールスマネージャーをしています。とても陽気で、友達が沢山います。ジョンは結婚しています。彼の奥さんの名前はアナ(Anna)です。彼女は私の義理の姉になります。ジョンとアナには息子がいます。その子の名前はジェイコブ(Jacob)で、3歳です。彼は私の甥です。

また、私には従妹が一人いて、ソフィア(Sophia)といいます。彼女はロサンゼルスに住んでいます。20歳です。髪はダークで、素晴らしい笑顔を持っています。サザンカリフォルニア大学の生徒です。独身ですが、彼がいます。彼の名前はジョナサン(Jonathan)です。かれはアーティストです。

私の祖母は70歳です。名前はエマ(Emma)です。退職しています。子供が二人いて、孫が三人います。彼女は、長女のイザベラ(Isabella)と一緒にヒューストンに住んでいます。私は彼女を毎月訪ねます。

Day
2

3. Dialogue

Listen to the audio and make sure you have clear understanding of the entire dialogue by looking at the mirror translation page.

Read the dialogue out loud. The dialogues just like texts should be read multiple times until you get to the point where you are satisfied with your reading and pronunciation. Remember, you don't have to achieve perfect pronunciation. Having distinguished accent is a good thing.

Now that you are satisfied with your reading try to record yourself reading the dialogue and compare your recording with the narrator's dialogue. Don't be disappointed if you hear that your reading is not as good as the narrators and don't spend too much time trying to perfect your pronunciation. Having accent is a good thing, remember?

Ethan: Hello, my name is Ethan.
William: I'm William. Nice to meet you.
Ethan: Nice to meet you, too, William. Where are you from?
William: I'm from Vancouver. And you?
Ethan: I'm from Toronto.

Michael: Hi, Daniel! How is everything?
Daniel: Not bad. How are you?
Michael: Pretty good, thanks. Have you met my friend Matthew?
Daniel: I don't think so.
Michael: Matthew, this is Daniel.
Daniel: Hello, Matthew.
Matthew: Hi, Daniel. Nice to meet you.
Michael: OK. We'll see you later.
Daniel: Bye-bye.

Receptionist: Hello. Are you a new student?
Emily: Yes, I am.
Receptionist: Sit down, then. I'm just going to ask you a few questions. What's your first name?
Emily: Emily.
Receptionist: And your last name?
Emily: Smith.
Receptionist: Smith. How do you spell it?
Emily: S-M-I-T-H.
Receptionist: And how old are you?
Emily: I'm 20.

3. ダイアローグ

音声を聞き、日本語のページを参照してダイアローグ全体の内容をしっかり理解して下さい。

ダイアローグを声に出して読んでください。ダイアローグはトピックの本文と同様、自分の音読と発音に満足するまで何度も何度も読み返して下さい。完璧な発音をする必要はありません。アクセントがあるという事は、あなたらしさがあるという事で、悪いことではありません。むしろ、良い事だと考えましょう。

自分の音読に満足したら、次はダイアローグを読んで録音してみましょう。完璧な発音を目指して時間をかけすぎる必要はありません。アクセントがあることは良い事でしたよね？

Ethan: こんにちは。私の名前はイーサン（Ethan）です。
William: 私はウィリアム（William）です。初めまして。
Ethan: 初めまして、ウィリアム。あなたは何処の出身ですか？
William: バンクーバー出身です。あなたは？
Ethan: 私はトロント出身です。

Michael: こんにちは、ダニエル（Daniel）。最近どう？
Daniel: 悪くないわ。あなたは元気？
Michael: まあまあ良いよ、ありがとう。僕の友達のマシュー（Matthew）に会ったことある？
Daniel: ないと思う。
Michael: Matthew、こちらは Danielだよ。
Daniel: こんにちは、Matthew。
Matthew: こんにちは、Daniel、初めまして。
Michael: オーケー、それじゃあ後でね。
Daniel: バイバイ。

受付：こんにちは。新しい生徒さんですか？
Emily: はい、そうです。
受付：それでは、お座りください。ちょっと質問を幾つかさせて頂きますね。下のお名前は何ですか？
Emily: エミリーです。
受付：それから、苗字は？
Emily: スミスです。
受付：スミスさんですね。スペルを教えてください。
Emily: S-M-I-T-H.
受付：何歳ですか？
Emily: はたち（20歳）です。

Receptionist: What is your address?
Emily: 356, East Victoria Way, Vancouver. The postal code is V5N6E1.
Receptionist: Perfect. What's your phone number?
Emily: My cell phone or my home phone number?
Receptionist: Both please.
Emily: My cell phone number is 555-994-6559, and my home phone number is 555-618-2317.
Receptionist: That's great, Emily. Thank you.

Day 2

4. Exercise

Read carefully each sentence and fill the blanks with missing words. All of the sentences that are used in your exercises are coming from texts and dialogues.

First read each sentence out loud (Remember ROLL?) filling in blanks.

With a pencil fill in the blanks with missing word and compare your words with those used in the dialogue or topic. Do not be disappointed if you make mistakes. It is all about the effort now.

a. I have an older sister, Jessica. She is 26. She has long black hair ____ black eyes.

b. I also ____ a cousin, Sophia. She lives in Los Angeles.

c. I am William. Nice __ meet you.

d. __ am an English teacher at Beijing Foreign Studies University.

e. John and Anna ____ a son. His name is Jacob, and he is 3 years old. He is my nephew.

受付：住所を教えてください。
Emily: バンクーバー市、イーストビクトリアウェイ３６５番です。郵便番号はV5N6E1です。
受付：分かりました。電話番号は何ですか？
Emily: ケータイですか、それとも家の電話ですか？
受付：両方お願いします。
Emily: ケータイのほうは555-994-6559で、家のほうは555-618-2317です。
受付：良いですね、エミリーさん。ありがとうございます。

二日目

4. エクササイズ

文をひとつひとつよく読んで、空白を埋めてください。この課題で使われた
文は全て、トピックとダイアローグで使われたものです。

> まず最初に、各文を声を出して読んで（ROLL学習法、覚えていますか？）、それか
> ら空白を埋めてください。
>
> 鉛筆を使って空白を埋め、自分の答えをダイアローグやトピックと比べて下さい。も
> し間違ってもがっかりしないで下さい。努力が肝心です。

a. I have an older sister, Jessica. She is 26. She has long black hair
____ black eyes.
b. I also _____ a cousin, Sophia. She lives in Los Angeles.
c. I am William. Nice ___ meet you.
d. ___ am an English teacher at Beijing Foreign Studies University.
e. John and Anna _____ a son. His name is Jacob, and he is 3 years
old. He is my nephew.

Day 3

1. Vocabulary

Review meaning of each word on mirror translation page. Do not be concerned if you don't completely understand the meaning of each one of the words.

Listen to the Day 3 audio file and read out loud each word in the Vocabulary section repeating each word after the narrator.

Repeat the process until you are satisfied with your reading and pronunciation.

It
For
Not
On
With
He
As
You
Do
At

2. Topic

Working with your topics is not going to get different from Day to Day. You need to follow the same routine every Day. I will have these instructions here once again.

First read through the text to gain some understanding of it by working with the mirror translation page. Don't hesitate to make marks right in the book with a pencil if you need to.

Read the entire text Out Loud as many times as it takes you to achieve flawless reading. You have to get to the stage where your reading gets easy and you don't have to pause between words and phrases.

三日目

1. ボキャブラリー

それぞれの単語の意味を日本語のページを見て確認して下さい。それぞれの単語の意味が完璧に分からなくても心配しないで下さい。

3日目の音声ファイルを聞いて、ボキャブラリーの部分にあるそれぞれの単語をナレーターについて声に出してリピートして下さい。

この作業をあなたの音読と発音に満足するまで続けてください。

It (それ)
For (〜のために)
Not (〜ではない(否定))
On (〜の上に(くっついている状態))
With (〜と共に)
He (彼は)
As (〜として)
You (あなたは)
Do (〜する)
At (〜で(場所・地点))

2. トピック

トピックへの取り組み方は日々で変わったりはしません。同じやり方を毎日しなくてはいけません。以下に再度、やり方を書いておきます。

最初に、ある程度理解するために、本文を日本語の部分と照らし合わせながら全て読みます。必要であれば、躊躇せずに、本に鉛筆などで印をつけてください。

本文全体を声に出して(Out Loud)何度でも完璧に読めるようになるまで繰り返し読んで下さい。読むのが簡単に感じられ、単語やフレーズで止まったりしなくても良くなる段階になるまで読んで下さい。

Listen to the audio provided with this lesson and compare your pronunciation with how it is pronounced by the narrator.

Remember what I said in Day 2? Reading the same text out loud over and over again works miracles. Yes, I am repeating myself - You have to read out loud the same text many times until it gets easy. You don't even have to put your brains to work here, just do mechanical reading of the same thing over and over again. You will be pleasantly surprised how great it works.

Day 3

James works as a librarian and lives with his son Aiden, aged 9. Here is his typical day.

6:30 I get up and make Aiden sandwiches. Then I do some housework. Then I wake up Aiden and make his breakfast. I'm always in a hurry and I don't have time for breakfast at home.
8:00 I put Aiden on a school bus and then cycle ten kilometers to work because the bus is expensive.
9:00 I have a sandwich for breakfast in the cafeteria, and then I start work. I like my job, but I don't earn much money and I have to stand almost all day.
5:00 I finish work and go to pick up Aiden. We go shopping.
6:30 I cook dinner and help Aiden with his homework. After dinner I do more housework or answer e-mails until nine. I don't go out in the evening because a babysitter is very expensive.
9:00 Aiden goes to bed and I read him a story. Then I go to bed – I'm really tired!

Alexander is a violinist in an orchestra. Here is his typical day.

I get up at about ten o'clock. I usually have breakfast in the garden. I have lunch at about two, and then I practice in the afternoon. Concerts usually start at eight, so I go to work at six thirty. I finish work at about ten thirty in the evening, and then I have dinner with friends. I get home after midnight. Then I watch TV or read a book, and go to bed at about two o'clock in the morning.

Liam is a senior in high school, and he has a part-time job as a cashier in a grocery store.

I work on Saturdays and Sundays from eight in the morning until four in the afternoon. I don't want to work on weeknights, because I need to study. I earn $8.50 an hour. It's not much money, but I save almost every penny! I want to go to a good university, and the cost goes up every year. Of course, I spend some money when I go out on Saturday nights.

このレッスンの音声を聞いて、ご自分の発音をナレーターの発音と比べて下さい。

私が2日目の中で言ったことを覚えていますか?同じ本文を何度も何度も声に出して読む事は奇跡のように効果があります。そうです、私はまた同じ事を言っているのです－簡単に感じられるようになるまで何度も同じ本文を読んで下さい。頭を働かせる必要さえありません、機械的に単純に何度も何度も読んで下さい。本当に素晴らしい効果があることに驚いて頂けると思います。

ジェームス(James)は、図書館司書で息子で9歳のアイドゥン(Aiden)と住んでいます。以下が彼の典型的な一日です。

6:30 私は起きて、Aidenのサンドイッチを作ります。それから、家事をします。
それからAidenを起こして、彼の朝食を作ります。私はいつも急がないといけないので、家で朝食を食べる時間はありません。
8:00 Aidenをスクールバスに乗せてから、私は10キロの道のりを仕事場まで自転車に乗ります、何故ならバス代が高いからです。
9:00 カフェテリアでサンドイッチを朝食に食べます、それから仕事を始めます。自分の仕事は好きですが、あまり沢山稼げませんし、ほぼ一日中立っていないといけません。
5:00 仕事を終え、Aidenを迎えに行きます。2人で買い物に行きます。
6:30 夕食を作ってAidenの宿題の手助けをします。夕食後は9時までまた家事をしたり、メールの返事を書いたりします。夜には出かけません、何故ならベビーシッターは高いからです。
9:00 Aidenがベッドに入り、私はAidenに本を読みます。それから私もベッドに入ります。本当に疲れた!

アレクサンダー(Alexander)は、オーケストラのバイオリン奏者です。以下が彼の典型的な一日です。

10時頃に起きます。通常は庭で朝食を食べます。昼食は2時ごろに食べて、それから午後は練習をします。コンサートは通常8時に始まるので、仕事には6時半に行きます。仕事を夜の10時半頃に終え、それから夕食は友人達と食べます。夜中の12時以降に家に帰ります。それからテレビを見たり本を読みます、そして、深夜2時頃に床に入ります。

リアム(Liam)は、高校3年生です、スーパーでキャッシャーをバイトとしています。

土曜と日曜は、朝の8時から夕方4時まで働きます。平日の夜は働きたくありません、何故なら勉強があるからです。時給は8ドル50セントです。あまり多くありませんが、全て貯金します!良い大学に行きたいのですが、学費は年々上がります。もちろん、土曜の夜に出かける時には幾らかお金は使います。

3. Dialogue

For your convenience, I am repeating the instructions at the beginning of this dialogue.

Listen to the audio and make sure you have clear understanding of the entire dialogue buy looking at the mirror translation page.

Read the dialogue out loud. The dialogues just like texts should be read multiple times until you get to the point where you are satisfied with your reading and pronunciation. Remember, you don't have to achieve perfect pronunciation. Having distinguished accent is a good thing.

Now that you are satisfied with your reading try to record yourself reading the dialogue. Don't spend too much time trying to perfect your pronunciation. Having accent is a good thing, remember?

Daily Routine

Anthony: How do you spend your day, Ben?
Benjamin: Well, on weekdays I get up around ten. Then I read the paper for an hour and have lunch at about noon.
A: Really? What time do you go to work?
B: I start work at three.
A: And when do you get home at night?
B: I get home pretty late, around midnight.
A: So what do you do, exactly?
B: I'm a TV announcer. Don't you recognize me?
A: No, I'm sorry. I don't watch TV.

Professor Wilson, a stress expert from the Simon Fraser University, looks at some people's typical day and tries to help...

Professor: Where do you work, Joshua?
J: I work for a computer company in Vancouver – but I live in Surrey.
P: So you travel from Surrey to Vancouver every day?
J: Yes. I drive 50 kilometers to work!
P: Do you always have breakfast?
J: No, I don't have time. I have to leave home at about half past seven.
P: What time do you start work?
J: At nine. I start work and I have a coffee. I drink about six cups of coffee a day.

3.ダイアローグ

あなたにとって便利なように、このダイアローグの最初にまた指示を書いておきますね。

音声を聞き、日本語のページを参照してダイアローグ全体の内容をしっかり理解して下さい。

ダイアローグを声に出して読んで下さい。トピックの本文のように、ダイアローグも自分の音読と発音に満足するまで何度でも読まなければなりません。ですが、忘れないで下さい、発音を完璧にする必要はないのです。他の人と違うあなたらしいアクセントがあるという事は良い事です。

自分の音読に満足したら、ダイアローグを読む自分の声を録音してみてください。発音を完璧にするために時間を取られ過ぎないで下さい。アクセントがある事は良い事でしたよね?

日課

アンソニー(Anthony): ベン、どんな風に一日を過ごすんだい?
ベンジャミン(Benjamin): えーと、平日は10時頃に起きるよ。それから新聞を1時間読んで、昼食は12時頃に食べるんだ。
A: 本当?何時に仕事に行くの?
B: 3時に仕事が始まるんだ。
A: それから何時に夜は家に帰るの?
B: かなり遅いね、夜中の12時ごろだな。
A: そうすると、仕事は具体的に何をしているの?
B: テレビのアナウンサーさ。僕の顔に見覚えがないかい?
A: ないなあ、ごめん。テレビ見ないんだ。

ウィルソン(Wilson)教授はサイモンフレイザー大学のストレス専門家で、人々の典型的な一日を見て、アドバイスをしている。。。

教授(Professor): ジョシュア(Joshua)、何処で働いているのですか?
J: バンクーバーでコンピュータ会社で働いています。ーだけど、私はサレーに住んでいます。
P: それじゃあ、サレーからバンクーバーまで毎日通勤しているのですか?
J: そうです。仕事まで50キロ運転します!
P: いつも朝食は食べますか?
J: いいえ、時間がないです。7時半頃には家を出ないといけないんです。
P: 何時に仕事は始まるのですか?
J: 9時です。働き始めたらコーヒーを飲みます。1日に6杯くらい飲みますね。

P: Do you go out for lunch?
J: No, I'm very busy. I have a sandwich in the office.
P: What time do you finish work?
J: I finish work at quarter to six. Then I drive back home.
P: Do you have dinner with your family?
J: No, I don't. My family has dinner at six. I don't get home until half past seven.
P: What do you do after dinner?
J: I sit and watch TV. I'm very tired. I usually go to sleep in front of the TV.
P: What time do you go to bed?
J: About eleven thirty.
P: Here is my advice. Have breakfast in the morning, Joshua, it's very important. But don't drink six cups of coffee – that's too much. Don't have lunch in the office, go out to a sandwich bar or restaurant. And finally, if possible find a new job in Surrey, not in Vancouver.

Day 3

4. Exercise

Read carefully each sentence and fill the blanks with missing words. All of the sentences that are used in your exercises are coming from texts and dialogues.

First read each sentence out loud (Remember ROLL?) filling in blanks.

With a pencil fill in the blanks with missing word and compare your words with those used in the dialogue or topic. Do not be disappointed if you make mistakes. It is all about the effort now.

a. I get up and make Aiden sandwiches. Then I __ some housework.
b. I put Aiden __ a school bus and then cycle ten kilometers to work because the bus is expensive.
c. I cook dinner and help Aiden ____ his homework.
d. I get up __ about ten o'clock.

P: 昼食には外に出ますか?
J: いいえ、とても忙しいんです。オフィスでサンドイッチを食べます。
P: 何時に仕事は終わりますか?
J: 6時の15分前に終わります。それから家までドライブします。
P: 夕食は家族と一緒ですか?
J: いいえ。家族は6時に夕食を食べます。私は7時半まで家に着きません。
P: 夕食後には何をしますか?
J: 座ってテレビを見ます。とても疲れています。いつもテレビの前で眠ってしまいます。
P: 何時にベッドに入りますか?
J: 11時半頃です。
P: これが私のアドバイスです。ジョシュア、朝ごはんを食べましょう。とても大切な事です。だけど、6杯もコーヒーは飲まないで下さいー多過ぎます。オフィスで昼食を食べないで、外に出てサンドイッチバーやレストランに行ってください。そして、最後に、出来るのであればサレーで仕事を見つけてください、バンクーバーではなく。

4. エクササイズ

各文を注意深く読んで、抜けている語を空白に埋めてください。このエクササイズで使われている文全ては、トピック本文とダイアローグから来ています。

まず最初に、各文を声を出して読んで(ROLL学習法、覚えていますか?)、それから空白を埋めてください。

鉛筆を使って空白を埋め、自分の答えをダイアローグやトピックと比べて下さい。もし間違ってもがっかりしないで下さい。努力が肝心です。

a. I get up and make Aiden sandwiches. Then I __ some housework.
b. I put Aiden __ a school bus and then cycle ten kilometers to work because the bus is expensive.
c. I cook dinner and help Aiden ____ his homework.
d. I get up __ about ten o'clock.

Day 4

1. Vocabulary

Review meaning of each word on mirror translation page. Do not be concerned if you don't completely understand the meaning of each one of the words.

Listen to the Day 4 audio file and read out loud each word in the Vocabulary section repeating each word after the narrator.

Repeat the process until you are satisfied with your reading and pronunciation.

This
But
His
By
From
They
We
Say
Her
She

Stealing an apple

THIS is **HIS** apple. **BUT BY** the time he comes back **FROM** school, **WE** can cut it to pieces and share it. **HIS** sister didn't **SAY** when he is coming back. He didn't tell **HER**. So **SHE** says we have to eat it quick.

2. Topic

Please follow the same routine that I presented in Working with Topic instructions in Day 2 and Day 3.

四日目

1. ボキャブラリー

それぞれの単語の意味を日本語のページを見て確認して下さい。それぞれの単語の意味が完璧に分からなくても心配しないで下さい。

4日目の音声ファイルを聞いて、ボキャブラリーの部分にあるそれぞれの単語をナレーターについて声に出してリピートして下さい。

この作業をあなたの音読と発音に満足するまで続けてください。

This (これは)
But (しかし)
His (彼の)
By (〜までには、〜によって)
From (〜から)
They (彼らは)
We (私たちは)
Say (言う)
Her (彼女に、彼女の)
She (彼女は)

りんごを盗むこと

これは、**彼の**りんごです。**しかし**、彼が学校**から**帰ってくる**までには**、**私たちは**そのりんごを幾つかに切って分け合うことが出来ます。**彼の**妹はいつ彼が帰って来るか**言い**ませんでした。彼は**彼女**に教えませんでした。**だから**、**彼女**は、私たちが急いで食べてしまわないといけないと言いました。

2. トピック

2日目と、3日目のトピック部分で私が提示したやり方に則って行なってください。

First read through the text to gain some understanding of it by working with the mirror translation page. Don't hesitate to make marks right in the book with a pencil if you need to.

Read the entire text Out Loud as many times as it takes you to achieve flawless reading. You have to get to the stage where your reading gets easy and you don't have to pause between words and phrases.

Listen to the audio provided with this lesson and compare your pronunciation with how it is pronounced by the narrator.

Please remember to **ROLL** from Day to Day.

Day 4

Homes around the world

Andrew from Seattle

I live in the old part of the town near the sea. I have a beautiful apartment. There's just one room in my apartment, one very big room with one very big window. My bed is next to the window so I see the sea and all the lights of the city when I go to sleep.

David from Philadelphia

Our house is quite old, about 50 years old but it still a very nice house. We have a living room, three bedrooms and a big kitchen. But the room we all love is a family room. There is a TV and a stereo and a large comfortable sofa in there, and some big, old armchairs. There is a rug under the coffee table, and there are always fresh flowers on the table. There are two plants on the floor next to the TV stand. There are a lot of pictures and photographs on the walls.

Joseph from Boston

My name is Joseph and I am from Boston. My house is fantastic. It's right next to the sea. My neighbors are very rich. Some of them are famous movie stars. In my house there are ten rooms, five are bedrooms, and everything is white – the floors, the walls, the doors, the sofas, everything. I also have a swimming pool, a home cinema and an exercise room. I live here alone.

最初に、ある程度理解するために、本文を日本語の部分と照らし合わせながら全て読みます。必要であれば、躊躇せずに、本に鉛筆などで印をつけてください。

本文全体を声に出して(Out Loud)何度でも完璧に読めるようになるまで繰り返し読んで下さい。読むのが簡単に感じられ、単語やフレーズで止まったりしなくても良くなる段階になるまで読んで下さい。

このレッスンの音声を聞いて、ご自分の発音をナレーターの発音と比べて下さい。

毎日、ROLLする (声に出して読む)ことを忘れないで下さい。

世界の家

四日目

シアトルに住むアンドリュー(Andrew)

私はこの街の、海に近い古いエリアに住んでいます。良いアパートに住んでいます。
アパートには部屋がひとつだけです、とても大きな部屋でとても大きな窓がひとつあります。
私のベッドは窓の隣なので眠りにつく時に海と街の明かりが全部見えます。

フィラデルフィアに住むディビッド(David)

私たちの家はかなり古いです、築50年くらいですが、まだとても良い家です。リビングがあり、ベッドルームが3つと、大きなキッチンがあります。だけど、私達みんなが大好きなのがファミリールームです。テレビとステレオ、それから大きくて心地良いソファーがそこにはあり、また、幾つかの大きくて古い肘掛け椅子もあります。コーヒーテーブルの下にはラグマットがあり、そのコーヒーテーブルにはいつも新しい花が飾ってあります。テレビスタンド横の床には鉢植えが2つあります。壁には沢山の絵や写真が飾ってあります。

ボストンに住むジョセフ(Joseph)

私の名前はジョセフで、ボストン出身です。私の家は素晴らしいです。海のすぐ隣です。近所の人たちはとてもお金持ちです。何人かは有名な映画スターです。私の家には部屋が10個あり、そのうち5つがベッドルームです、そして全てが白が基調です。ー床、壁、ドア、ソファー、全て。それから、プールに、映画用の部屋と、エクササイズ用の部屋もあります。私は一人で住んでいます。

Rules for Tenants

1. The rent is due on the first of every month.
2. No pets are allowed.
3. Parking is in numbered stalls only. Guests should park on the street. Don't drive or park on grass.
4. Trash pickup is on Thursdays. Recycle glass, plastic, aluminum, and paper. Put trash in plastic bags or trash cans. Don't litter.
5. Don't make loud noise between 11 pm and 9 am.
6. Laundry room is for tenants only. Please don't use a clotheslines on the balcony. Use the dryer in the laundry room.
7. Don't use a barbecue inside. Use it only in the patio or on the balcony. Don't use it for longer than two hours, twice a day.
8. Live Christmas trees are not allowed.

Day
4

3. Dialogue

Here I repeat the same instructions once more so you don't have to flip between pages.

Listen to the audio and make sure you have clear understanding of the entire dialogue by looking at the mirror translation page.

Read the dialogue out loud. The dialogues just like texts should be read multiple times until you get to the point where you are satisfied with your reading and pronunciation. Remember, you don't have to achieve perfect pronunciation. Having distinguished accent is a good thing.

Now that you are satisfied with your reading try to record yourself reading the dialogue and compare your recording with narrators dialogue. Don't be disappointed if you hear that your reading is not as good as narrators and don't spend too much time trying to perfect your pronunciation. Having accent is a good thing, remember?

借家人規定

1．毎月1日が家賃の支払期日です。
2．ペットは飼ってはいけません。
3．駐車は数字が書いてある区画のみです。来客は路上に駐車してください。芝生の上で車を走らせたり、駐車しないで下さい。
4．　ごみの日は木曜日です。ガラスとプラスチック、アルミ、紙をリサイクルしてください。ごみはビニールの袋か、（ゴミ捨て場にある）大きなゴミ入れに入れてください。散らかさないで下さい。
5．午後11時から朝の9時までは騒音を出さないで下さい。
6．洗濯室は借家人用のみです。バルコニーで物干し用ロープを使わないで下さい。洗濯室にある乾燥機を使ってください。
7．　バーベキューを室内で使用しないで下さい。パティオやバルコニーでのみ使ってください。1日2回以上、2時間以上使わないで下さい。
8．クリスマスツリーは本物の木は許可されていません。

四日目

3. ダイアローグ

ここに同じ指示を書いておきます、そうすればページを遡って見なくて済みますね。

音声を聞き、日本語のページを参照してダイアローグ全体の内容をしっかり理解して下さい。

ダイアローグを声に出して読んでください。ダイアローグはトピックの本文と同様、自分の音読と発音に満足するまで何度も何度も読み返して下さい。完璧な発音をする必要はありません。アクセントがあるという事は、あなたらしさがあるという事で、悪いことではありません。むしろ、良い事だと考えましょう。

自分の音読に満足したら、次はダイアローグを読んで録音してみましょう。完璧な発音を目指して時間をかけすぎる必要はありません。アクセントがあることは良い事でしたよね？

Ella: Well, what do you think about this apartment?

Jack: It is bright and modern. There are two bedrooms, and the living room is quite big.

E: But the bedrooms are too small. And there isn't enough closet space for my clothes. The last apartment we saw was much bigger.

J: But it was older and darker. This one is on the eleventh floor. It has big windows and a balcony overlooking the city. The view is magnificent! My friend Ashely likes it very much. She likes to have an apartment with a view.

E: I don't like high-rises. The last apartment was on the first floor and had a private patio.

J: This apartment has two bathrooms.

E: But there are no windows in the kitchen. And there is no room for a table there.

J: There are two parking spaces here. The last apartment had only one.

E: The last apartment was less expensive.

J: But it was far from the city centre. This apartment is in Centre Street.

E: But this neighborhood is more dangerous.

J: OK, let's ask the real estate agent to show us something else.

Chris: Excuse me. I'm your new neighbor, Chris. I've just moved in.

Dan: Oh, hi. I'm Dan. Do you need any help?

C: I'm looking for a grocery store. Are there any around here?

D: Yes, there are some on Robson Street.

C: And is there a Laundromat near here?

D: No, but there is a laundry room downstairs.

C: Do you know any good Italian restaurant in the neighborhood?

D: Yes, there is a great one a couple of blocks from here.

C: OK. And where is the closest post office?

D: I think there is one in the shopping mall.

C: Thank you.

D: By the way, there is a barber's shop in the shopping mall, too.

C: A barber's shop?

エラ(Ella)：えーと、このアパートどう思う？
ジャック(Jack)：明るくてモダンだね。ベッドルームが2つあって、リビングはかなり大きいね。
E: ベッドルームはどちらも小さ過ぎるわ。私の服にはクローゼットのスペースが十分じゃないし。最後に見たアパートはもっと大きかったわ。
J: だけど、あれはもっと古くて暗かったね。こっちのアパートの部屋は11階にあるよ。窓が大きくてバルコニーは市内を見渡せるよ。眺めは本当に素晴らしいよ！僕の友達のアシュリー(Ashely)はここが大好きだってさ。彼女は眺めが良いアパートに住みたいんだ。
E: 高層ビルは好きじゃないわ。最後に見たアパートは1階で自分だけの中庭があるわ。
J: このアパートはバスルームが2つあるよ。
E: だけど、キッチンに窓がないわ。それにテーブルを置くスペースもない。
J: ここには駐車スペースが2つあるよ。最後に見たアパートには1つしかない。
E: 最後に見たアパートはもっと安かったわ。
J: だけど、市の中心部からは遠いね。このアパートはセンターストリートにあるよ。
E: だけど、この近所のほうが安全じゃないわ。
J: わかったよ、不動産屋に違う物件を見せてもらおう。

四日目

クリス(Chris)： すみません。新しい隣人のクリスです。ちょうど引っ越したところです。
ダン(Dan)：ああ、こんにちは。ダンです。お手伝いしましょうか？
C: スーパーを探してるんですが。この辺にありますか？
D: はい、ロブソンストリートに幾つかありますよ。
C: この辺りにコインランドリーはありますか？
D: いいえ、だけど洗濯室は下の階にありますよ。
C: この近所に美味しいイタリアンレストランがあるか知ってますか？
D: はい、ここから2ブロックの所にすごく良いのがありますよ。
C: オーケー、それから何処が一番近い郵便局ですか？
D: そのショッピングモールにあると思いますよ。
C: ありがとうございます。
D: ところで、床屋もそのモールにありますよ。
C: 床屋ですか？

4. Exercise

Read carefully each sentence and fill the blanks with missing words. All of the sentences that are used in your exercises are coming from texts and dialogues.

Read each sentence out loud (remember ROLL?) .

With a pencil fill in the blanks with missing words and compare your words with those used in the dialogue or topic. Do not be disappointed if you make mistakes. It is all about the effort now.

Day 4

Remember Stealing an apple sentence?

_____ is ___ apple, ___ _____ the time he comes back _____ school __ can cut it to pieces and share it. _____ sister didn't _____ when he is coming back. He didn't tell _____. So _____ says we have to eat it quick.

4. エクササイズ

各文を注意深く読んで、抜けている語を空白に埋めてください。このエクササイズで使われている文全ては、トピック本文とダイアローグから来ています。

まず最初に、各文を声を出して読んで(ROLL学習法、覚えていますか?)

鉛筆を使って空白を埋め、自分の答えをダイアローグやトピックと比べて下さい。もし間違ってもがっかりしないで下さい。努力が肝心です。

「りんごを盗むこと」の文を覚えてますか?

_____ is ___ apple, ___ _____ the time he comes back _____ school __ can cut it to pieces and share it. _____ sister didn't _____ when he is coming back. He didn't tell _____. So _____ says we have to eat it quick.

Day 5

1. Vocabulary

Review meaning of each word on mirror translation page. Do not be concerned if you don't completely understand the meaning of each one of the words.

Listen to the Day 5 audio file and read out loud each word in the Vocabulary section repeating each word after the narrator.

Repeat the process until you are satisfied with your reading and pronunciation.

Or
An
Will
My
One
All
Would
There
Their
What

2. Topic

Please follow the same routine that I presented in Working with Topic instructions in Day 2 and Day 3.

First read through the text to gain some understanding of it by working with the mirror translation page. Don't hesitate to make marks right in the book with a pencil if you need to.

Read the entire text Out Loud as many times as it takes you to achieve flawless reading. You have to get to the stage where your reading gets easy and you don't have to pause between words and phrases.

Listen to the audio provided with this lesson and compare your pronunciation with how it is pronounced by the narrator.

五日目

1. ボキャブラリー

それぞれの単語の意味を日本語のページを見て確認して下さい。それぞれの単語の意味が完璧に分からなくても心配しないで下さい。

5日目の音声ファイルを聞いて、ボキャブラリーの部分にあるそれぞれの単語をナレーターについて声に出してリピートして下さい。

この作業をあなたの音読と発音に満足するまで続けてください。

Or (または)

An (ひとつの)

Will (〜でしょう(未来))

My (私の)

One (いち)

All (全て)

Would (〜だろう(willの過去形)、〜するつもりだ)

There (そこに)

Their (彼らの)

What (何)

2. トピック

2日目と、3日目のトピック部分で私が提示したやり方に則って行なってください。

最初に、ある程度理解するために、本文を日本語の部分と照らし合わせながら全て読みます。必要であれば、躊躇せずに、本に鉛筆などで印をつけてください。

本文全体を声に出して(Out Loud)何度でも完璧に読めるようになるまで繰り返し読んで下さい。読むのが簡単に感じられ、単語やフレーズで止まったりしなくても良くなる段階になるまで読んで下さい。

このレッスンの音声を聞いて、ご自分の発音をナレーターの発音と比べて下さい。

Please remember to **ROLL** from Day to Day.

Healthy Eating!

Do you want to be healthy? Perhaps you need to go on a diet.
- Start the day with a glass of water or orange juice … but no coffee or tea, and no milk or sugar, please!
- For lunch, don't eat any fried foods, such as French fries, or burgers … some grilled fish, perhaps with some green vegetables, is really good for you! An apple is always a good choice.
- Do you want some pasta for lunch? OK, but don't put any cheese or white sauce on top! Tomato sauce is much better.
- Don't eat any desserts that contain cream, butter, or chocolate!
- If you're still hungry, eat some fruit, or have some nuts – they are really healthy!
- And to drink … just water! It doesn't have any calories so you can drink as much as you want.
- For dinner, have some soup and bread. It's simple … but delicious!

Day 5

3. Dialogue

I am sure you now are quite familiar with what you need to do, so I can change the instructions into a short reminders, it will now work well for you.

Listen to the audio and make sure you understand the dialogue clearly.

Read the dialogue out loud as many times as it takes until you are satisfied with the result.

Record yourself reading the dialogue.

Ordering a Meal

Waiter: Good morning. Can I help you?
Customer: Yes, I would like a ham sandwich. Do you have rye bread?
W: Yes. Would you like lettuce and tomato on your sandwich?
C: Please. And I want the bread toasted. And a little mayonnaise, too.
W: Anything to drink?
C: Coffee, please.
W: Would you like any cream or sugar with your coffee?

日々、**ROLL**する事を忘れないでください。

健康的な食生活！

健康になりたいですか？もしかするとあなたはダイエットする必要があるかも知れません。
－　1日の始めに水やオレンジジュースを飲みましょう。。。でも、コーヒーやお茶はだめ、そしてミルクや砂糖もなしでお願いします！
－　昼食には、ハンバーガーやフライドポテトなど、油を使った料理を食べないでください。焼き魚や、緑の野菜が本当に体に良いです！りんごはいつでも良いチョイスです。
－　パスタを昼食に食べたいですか？オーケー、でもチーズやホワイトソースはかけないでください！トマトソースの方がずっと良いです。
－　クリームや、バター、またはチョコレートが入っているデザートを食べないでください！
－　それでもお腹が空いてるなら、フルーツやナッツを食べてください－フルーツやナッツはとても健康に良いです！
－　それから飲み物は。。。水だけです！全くカロリーがないから、飲みたいだけ飲めます。
－　夕食には、スープとパンを食べてください。シンプル。。。だけど、美味しいです！

3. ダイアローグ

五日目

もうきっと、何をすれば良いのかよく分かって頂けていると思います、なのでその指示を短いリマインダーにします、それでもよく分かって頂けるでしょう。

音声を聞いて、ダイアローグの内容をはっきり理解しているか確認して下さい。

満足するまで何度でもダイアローグを声に出して読んで下さい。

ダイアローグを読む自分の声を録音してください。

食事をオーダーする

ウェイター（Waiter）: おはようございます。何になさいますか？
客（Customer）: はい、ハムサンドイッチをお願いします。ライ麦パンはありますか？
W: はい。サンドイッチにはレタスとトマトをお入れしますか？
C: お願いします。パンは焼いてください。それから、マヨネーズを少しお願いします。
W: お飲み物は？
C: コーヒーをお願いします。
W: コーヒーにクリームや砂糖は必要ですか？

C: Yes please, one milk and one sugar.
W: For here or to go?
C: For here. How much is that?
W: Four dollars ninety-five cents, please.

Hostess: Good evening!
Customer: Good evening! We'd like a table for two by the window, please.
H: Certainly, please follow me.
C: Thank you very much. Can we have the menu, please?
H: Here it is.

Waiter: Are you ready to order?
A: Yes. I'd like the steak with mashed potatoes, please.
W: How do you want the steak – rare, medium or well done?
A: Well done, please.
B: And I'll have the grilled salmon and a mixed salad with Italian dressing.
W: What would you like to drink?
A: I'll have a glass of red wine. They say red wine is good for you.
B: Just an iced tea for me, please.
W: OK. Coming right up.

Day
5

W: Would you like a dessert?
A: Yes, please. What do you have?
W: Tiramisu, ice cream or fruit salad.
A: Fruit salad, please.
B: Nothing for me, thanks.
A: And can we have the check, please?

MENU

Appetizers			Desserts		
* Garlic Bread	1.50		* Apple Pie	2.95	
* Fried Calamari	4.50		* Banana Split	5.95	
			* Vanilla Ice Cream	4.95	
Salads					
			Drinks		
* Caesar Salad	3.95				
* Garden Salad	2.95		* Cola/Iced Tea		
			Small	1.95	
Entrees			* Juice		
			Large	2.50	
* Sirloin Steak	9.95		* Beer	4.95	
* Roast Chicken	11.95		* Wine	6.50	
* Deluxe Burger	6.95		* Coffee	3.95	

C: はい、お願いします、ミルクと砂糖をひとつずつ。
W: こちらでお召し上がりですか、お持ち帰りですか?
C: ここで食べていきます。おいくらですか?
W: 4ドル95セントです。

ホステス(客席までの案内係)(Hostess): こんばんは。
客(Customer): こんばんは。窓際の2人用の席をお願いしたいんですが。
H: かしこまりました、どうぞついて来てください。
C: ありがとうございます。メニューを頂けますか?
H: はいどうぞ。

Waiter: ご注文はお決まりですか?
A: はい。マッシュドポテトがついているこのステーキをお願いします。
W: ステーキの焼き加減は?ーレア、ミディアム、ウェルダン?
A: ウェルダンをお願いします。
B: 私はサーモングリルとミックスサラダをイタリアンドレッシングつきでお願いします。
W: お飲み物は?
A: 赤ワインを一杯おねがいします。赤ワインは体に良いっていうから。
B: 私にはアイスティーをお願いします。
W: 分かりました。すぐにお持ちします。

W: デザートはいかがですか?
A: はい、頂きます。どんなデザートがありますか?
W: ティラミス、アイスクリームとフルーツサラダです。
A: フルーツサラダをお願いします。
B: わたしはいいです。
A: お勘定もお願いします。

五日目

メニュー

前菜
* ガーリックブレッド 1.50
* 揚げカラマリ 4.50

サラダ
* シーザーサラダ 3.95
* ガーデンサラダ 2.95

主菜
* サーロインステーキ 9.95
* ローストチキン 11.95
* デラックスバーガー 6.95

デザート
* アップルパイ 2.95
* バナナスプリット 5.95
* バニラアイスクリーム 4.95

ドリンク
* コーラまたはアイスティー Sサイズ 1.95
* ジュース Lサイズ 2.50
* ビール 4.95
* ワイン 6.50
* コーヒー 3.95

4. Exercise

From now on your exercise sentences will be completely irrelevant to the content of your topics or dialogues but will concentrate on the vocabulary part of your Day. Read carefully each sentence and fill the blanks with missing words from your Vocabulary.

Read each sentence out loud (remember ROLL?) .

With a pencil fill in the blanks with missing words and compare your words with those used in the dialogue or topic. Do not be disappointed if you make mistakes. It is all about the effort now.

a. What movies do you like better, drama ___ comedy?

b. The manager wants to see you at noon. ____ you be able to make it on time?

c. The summer is ___ favorite season.

d. I have seen this movie only ____ time. I _____ like to see it again.

e. ____ movies do you like better, drama or comedy?

4. エクササイズ

この日以降は、エクササイズの文はトピック本文やダイアローグとは全く関連がなくなりますが、その日のボキャブラリーに焦点が置かれます。各文を注意深く読み、足りない語をボキャブラリーから空白に補ってください。

まず最初に、各文を声を出して読んで(ROLL学習法、覚えていますか?)

鉛筆を使って空白を埋め、自分の答えをダイアローグやトピックと比べて下さい。もし間違ってもがっかりしないで下さい。努力が肝心です。

五日目

a. What movies do you like better, drama ____ comedy?
b. The manager wants to see you at noon. ____ you be able to make it on time?
c. The summer is ____ favorite season.
d. I have seen this movie only ____ time. I ____ like to see it again.
e. ____ movies do you like better, drama or comedy?

Day 6

1. Vocabulary

Review meaning of each word on mirror translation page. Do not be concerned if you don't completely understand the meaning of each one of the words.

Listen to the Day 6 audio file and read out loud each word in the Vocabulary section repeating each word after the narrator.

Repeat the process until you are satisfied with your reading and pronunciation.

So
Up
Out
If
About
Who
Get
Which
Go
Me

2. Topic

Please follow the same routine that I presented in Working with Topic instructions in Day 2 and Day 3.

First read through the text to gain some understanding of it by working with the mirror translation page. Don't hesitate to make marks right in the book with a pencil if you need to.

Read the entire text Out Loud as many times as it takes you to achieve flawless reading. You have to get to the stage where your reading gets easy and you don't have to pause between words and phrases.

Listen to the audio provided with this lesson and compare your pronunciation with how it is pronounced by the narrator.

六日目

1. ボキャブラリー

それぞれの単語の意味を日本語のページを見て確認して下さい。それぞれの単語の意味が完璧に分からなくても心配しないで下さい。

6日目の音声ファイルを聞いて、ボキャブラリーの部分にあるそれぞれの単語をナレーターについて声に出してリピートして下さい。

この作業をあなたの音読と発音に満足するまで続けてください。

So (とても)
Up (上に)
Out (外に)
If (もし)
About (〜について)
Who (誰)
Get (得る)
Which (どちら)
Go (行く)
Me (私(に))

2. トピック

2日目と、3日目のトピック部分で私が提示したやり方に則って行なってください。

最初に、ある程度理解するために、本文を日本語の部分と照らし合わせながら全て読みます。必要であれば、躊躇せずに、本に鉛筆などで印をつけてください。

本文全体を声に出して(Out Loud)何度でも完璧に読めるようになるまで繰り返し読んで下さい。読むのが簡単に感じられ、単語やフレーズで止まったりしなくても良くなる段階になるまで読んで下さい。

このレッスンの音声を聞いて、ご自分の発音をナレーターの発音と比べて下さい。

Please remember to **ROLL** from Day to Day.

Phone Service

When you move to a new apartment, you need to apply for phone service. Call the local phone company for the phone connection or order it over the Internet. Many people have answering machines or voice mail. When you hear the message, wait for the beep. After the beep, leave your name, phone number and a message.

You can get long-distance service from many different companies. Their rates differ very much. Or you can use pre-paid phone cards to call overseas. To use a phone card, dial the number on the card. It may be cheaper to make long-distance calls on weekends, evenings and on some holidays.

A local phone call from a pay phone costs 25 cents per call. If you don't have coins, you can dial 0 and tell the operator that you want to "call collect" – the person you're calling will pay for the call.

Telephone numbers beginnings with 1-800, 1-888, or 1-877 are "toll free" numbers. You don't need to pay for the call. Telephone numbers beginnings with 1-900 are "pay per call" numbers. You will have to pay for them. These calls are often very expensive.

If you need any help with a phone call, dial 0 for the operator.

You can also buy a cell phone. It is very easy to use. First of all, don't forget to turn it on. Then dial the number and remember to press the "Call" button. Make sure to recharge the batteries every few days. Try not to drop the phone – it's fragile. And don't forget to pay the phone bill every month.

Day 6

Getting Online

If you like to browse the Web and use e-mail, you need to get an Internet connection. First choose the type of connection – ADSL or cable. Then compare Internet Service Providers (ISPs) operating in your area. ISPs have different service plans and rates. Select the provider that is best for you. Then sign up with the ISP. The ISP will help you set up the connection and get online.

日々、**ROLL**する事を忘れないでください。

電話サービス

アパートに引っ越したら、電話サービスに申し込む必要があります。地域の電話会社に電話して電話接続を頼んだり、または、インターネットで頼んでください。多くの人は留守番電話機や、ボイスメールを持っています。メッセージが聞こえたら、ピーッという音を待って下さい。その音の後に、自分の名前と電話番号とメッセージを残します。

沢山の色んな会社から長距離電話のサービスを受けることができます。彼らの料金は様々です。また、プリペイドのフォーンカードを使って海外にかけることもできます。フォーンカードを使うには、カードに載っている番号にかけます。週末、夜や、ホリデー中にかけると安いかもしれません。

公衆電話から自分のいる地域内でかけるには25セントかかります。コインを持っていなければ、0番にかけて、オペレーターに「コレクトコール」をかけたいと伝えます。－電話の相手側が払うことになります。

1-800、1-888、1-877で始まる番号は「フリーダイアル」の番号です。あなたは料金を支払いません。1-900で始まる番号は、「ペイ・パー・コール」の番号です。あなたが電話料金を払わなくてはなりません。こういった通話は大抵とても高いです。

もしアシスタントが必要であれば、0番をかければオペレーターが出ます。

また、携帯電話も買えます。使い方は簡単です。まず始めに、スイッチを入れるのを忘れないで下さい。それから、番号をかけますが、「送信」ボタンを押すのを忘れないでください。何日かおきにバッテリーを充電するのを忘れないようにしましょう。落とさないようにして下さい－壊れ易いです。それから、毎月の電話代を払うのを忘れないようにしましょう。

六日日

インターネットに接続

ウェブサイトを見たかったり、電子メールを使いたければ、インターネット接続をしなければなりません。最初に接続のタイプを選びます。－ADSLかケーブルです。それから自分の地域のインターネットサービスプロバイダー(ISPs)を比較します。ISPsには、色々なサービスプランや料金形態があります。あなたに一番合ったプロバイダーを選んで下さい。その後、そのISPと契約をします。あなたのISPは、インターネット接続のセットアップを手伝ってくれます。

3. Dialogue

Listen to the audio and make sure you understand the dialogue clearly.

Read the dialogue out loud as many times as it takes until you are satisfied with the result.

Record yourself reading the dialogue.

Telephone Conversation

Manager's Office: Hello, Manager's Office speaking.
Ryan: Good morning, I'd like to talk to Mr. Green, please.
MO: Hold on, please, I'll find out if he is in.
R: All right.
MO: ... Sorry, but Mr. Green is out. Can I take a message?
R: May I call back later?
MO: Certainly. Please call back after 3 pm.
R: Thank you. Good-bye!

A: Hello!
B: Hi, may I speak to Lily please?
A: I'm afraid you have the wrong number. What number are you calling?
B: I'm calling 320-4565.
A: This is 320-4565, but there is no one by the name Lily here.
B: I'm sorry.
A: That's all right.

A: Good afternoon, Peach Computer Services. Can I help you?
B: Yes. Do you sell laptops?
A: Yes, we do.
B: Great! What are your hours?
A: We're open from 9 to 6.
B: Thanks a lot. Bye.

Lucas: Hello.
John: Hello, is Natalie there?
Lucas: Yes, just a minute. I'll get her... Natalie, it's for you.
Natalie: Hello.
John: Hi, Natalie. This is John. Would you like to go to a movie tonight?
Lucas: Thanks, I'd love to.
John: Good. I'll pick you up at around seven-thirty.
Natalie: Fine. I'll be ready.
John: See you then. Bye.

3. ダイアローグ

音声を聞いて、ダイアローグの内容をはっきり理解しているか確認して下さい。

満足するまで何度でもダイアローグを声に出して読んで下さい。

ダイアローグを読む自分の声を録音してください。

電話の会話

マネージャーのオフィス (Manager's Office): もしもし、マネージャーのオフィスです。
Ryan: おはようございます。グリーンさんとお話したいのですが。
MO: お待ちください。オフィスにいるか確かめます。
R: 分かりました。
MO: 残念ですが、グリーンさんは外に出ています。メッセージを頂きましょうか？
R: 後ほどおかけ直しして良いですか？
MO: もちろんです。午後3時以降におかけください。
R: ありがとうございます。さようなら。

A: もしもし。
B: もしもし、リリーさんとお話できますか？
A: 残念ですが番号が間違っています。何番におかけですか？
B: 320-4565にかけています。
A: こちらは320-4565ですけど、リリーという名前の人はいません。
B: 済みません。
A: 大丈夫ですよ。

A: こんにちは、ピーチコンピューターサービスです。ご用件は？
B: はい。ラップトップは売っていますか？
A: はい、売っております。
B: 良かった！何時から何時まで開いていますか？
A: 9時から6時まで開いています。
B: 本当にありがとう。バーイ。

Lucas: もしもし。
John: もしもし、ナタリーはいますか？
Lucas: はい、ちょっと待って。呼んで来ます。。ナタリー、電話だよ。
Natalie: もしもし。
John: もしもし、ナタリー。ジョンだよ。今晩映画に行かない？
Lucas: ありがとう、行きたいわ。
John: 良かった。7時半に迎えに行くよ。
Natalie: いいわ。準備しておくね。
John: じゃあその時にね。バーイ。

4. Exercise

ROLL AWAY !

Your exercise sentences are now completely irrelevant of the content of your topics or dialogues but will concentrate only on vocabulary part of your Day. Read carefully each sentence and fill in the blank spaces with missing words from your Vocabulary.

Read each sentence out loud (remember ROLL?) .

With a pencil fill in the blanks with missing words and compare your words with those used in the dialogue or topic.

Day 6

a. Learning English is not easy and it takes ___ much effort. It is __ important to understand.

b. Please put the book ___ on the top shelf.

c. Can you please pull the key ___ of the lock?

d. ___ you are hot you should drink some water.

e. Can you tell me _____ sailing? Is it fun?

f. Do you know _____ is the manager in this book store?

g. This is out stop, we need to ___ off the bus.

h. You read both of these books? _____ one did you like better?

i. I have to ____ back to my class. I don't want to be late.

j. My girlfriend bought this English book for____. She wants me to learn English.

4. エクササイズ

沢山ROLLしてください!

エクササイズの文はトピック本文やダイアローグとはもう関連がないですが、その日のボキャブラリーに焦点が置かれています。各文を注意深く読み、足りない語をボキャブラリーから空白に補ってください。

まず最初に、各文を声を出して読んで(ROLL学習法、覚えていますか?)

鉛筆を使って空白を埋め、自分の答えをダイアローグやトピックと比べて下さい。

a. Learning English is not easy and it takes ___ much effort. It is __ important to understand.

b. Please put the book ___ on the top shelf.

c. Can you please pull the key ___ of the lock?

d. ___ you are hot you should drink some water.

e. Can you tell me _____ sailing? Is it fun?

f. Do you know _____ is the manager in this book store?

g. This is out stop, we need to ___ off the bus.

h. You read both of these books? _____ one did you like better?

i. I have to _____ back to my class. I don't want to be late.

j. My girlfriend bought this English book for_____. She wants me to learn English.

六
日
目

Day 7

1. Vocabulary

Review meaning of each word on mirror translation page. Do not be concerned if you don't completely understand the meaning of each one of the words.

Listen to the Day 7 audio file and read out loud each word in the Vocabulary section repeating each word after the narrator.

Repeat the process until you are satisfied with your reading and pronunciation.

When
Make
Can
Like
Time
No
Just
Him
Know
Take

2. Topic

Please follow the same routine that I presented in Working with Topic instructions in Day 2 and Day 3.

First read through the text to gain some understanding of it by working with the mirror translation page. Don't hesitate to make marks right in the book with a pencil if you need to.

Read the entire text Out Loud as many times as it takes you to achieve flawless reading. You have to get to the stage where your reading gets easy and you don't have to pause between words and phrases.

Listen to the audio provided with this lesson and compare your pronunciation with how it is pronounced by the narrator.

七日目

1. ボキャブラリー

それぞれの単語の意味を日本語のページを見て確認して下さい。それぞれの単語の意味が完璧に分からなくても心配しないで下さい。

7日目の音声ファイルを聞いて、ボキャブラリーの部分にあるそれぞれの単語をナレーターについて声に出してリピートして下さい。

この作業をあなたの音読と発音に満足するまで続けてください。

When (いつ、時)
Make (作る)
Can (できる、可能)
Like (好き、〜のような)
Time (時間)
No (いいえ)
Just (ただ、単に)
Him (彼に)
Know (知っている)
Take (持っていく、連れて行く)

2. トピック

2日目と、3日目のトピック部分で私が提示したやり方に則って行なってください。

最初に、ある程度理解するために、本文を日本語の部分と照らし合わせながら全て読みます。必要であれば、躊躇せずに、本に鉛筆などで印をつけてください。

本文全体を声に出して(Out Loud)何度でも完璧に読めるようになるまで繰り返し読んで下さい。読むのが簡単に感じられ、単語やフレーズで止まったりしなくても良くなる段階になるまで読んで下さい。

このレッスンの音声を聞いて、ご自分の発音をナレーターの発音と比べて下さい。

Please remember to **ROLL** from Day to Day.

TV Ad

Hello. This is Martin Thompson, owner of Martin's Clothing. All of us here at Martin's Clothing are very proud of our store. At Martin's, there are clothes and accessories for everyone. Are you looking for a hat? Or maybe a belt? How about a sweater or a jacket? What about an umbrella for those rainy days? Are you looking for a necklace as a gift for a special person? What about a soft woolen scarf or leather gloves? Well, come on over to Martin's, where there're lots of hats, belts, sweaters, jackets, umbrellas, necklaces, scarves, and gloves. So take it from me, Martin Thompson. At Martin's, there is clothing for everyone.

Shopping: Men and Women are Different

It's not only women who love shopping – today men like it too. Some men say it's their favorite hobby. But men and women shop in very different ways...

Where do they go?
Women: Clothes shops, clothes shops, more clothes shops.
Men: Clothes shops, electronics shops, music shops.

Day 7

How long do they spend shopping?
Men: An hour, possibly two.
Women: A day.

What do they love?
Women: They love looking at everything, trying on clothes, and talking to the shop assistants.
Men: They love getting home! They love trying on their new clothes and playing with their new "toys."

What do they hate?
Men: They hate waiting for women to decide what they want. They hate asking shop assistants for help.
Women: They hate hearing "Can we go home now? The football starts in half an hour."

日々、**ROLL**する事を忘れないでください。

テレビ広告

こんにちは。マーティン・トンプソン(Martin Thompson)と申しまして、マーティン洋服店のオーナーです。私共従業員は皆、この店を誇りに思っています。マーティン洋服店には、みなさんに気に入って頂ける服やアクセサリーがあります。帽子をお探しですか？それともベルトですか？セーターやジャケットはいかがですか？雨の日に傘はどうですか？特別な人へのギフトにネックレスをお探しですか？柔らかいウールのスカーフや革の手袋はいかがですか？帽子、ベルト、セーター、ジャケット、傘、ネックレス、スカーフや手袋が沢山あるマーティン洋服店にどうぞお越しください。私、マーティン・トンプソンが保証します。マーティン洋服店にはみなさんの気に入る衣類があります。

ショッピング：男と女は違う

ショッピングが好きなのは女性だけではありません。－今日では男性もショッピングが好きです。ショッピングが一番の趣味という男性もいます。ですが、男性と女性ではショッピングの仕方がとても違います。

どこに行くか？
女性：洋服屋、洋服屋、そしてまた洋服屋。
男性：洋服屋、電気屋、ミュージックショップ。

どのくらいショッピングに時間をかけるか？
男性：1時間、場合によって2時間。
女性：1日中。

何が好きか？
女性：何でも見るのが好き、試着すること、店員と話をすること。
男性：家に帰ること！新しい服を着て、新しい遊び道具で遊ぶ事。

何が嫌いか？
男性：女性が何を買うか決めるまで待っている事。店員に助けを求めること。
女性：「もう家に帰ろうよ。フットボールが30分後に始まるから」と聞く事。

七日目

85

3. Dialogue

Listen to the audio and make sure you understand the dialogue clearly.

Read the dialogue out loud as many times as it takes until you are satisfied with the result.

Record yourself reading the dialogue.

Shopping

A: Let's take a shopping cart. We have a long shopping list today.
B: Sure. Let's start with dairy products. We need a pound of unsalted butter, a carton of skimmed milk, and a dozen eggs.
A: These eggs come in a lot of sizes: small, medium, large, extra-large, and jumbo.
B: Let's get the large size. They're on sale.
A: OK. What's next?
B: Half a pound of cheese, a jar of pickles, and a couple tins of tuna.
A: Here you are. Do we need any fruits or vegetables?
B: Yes, let's go to the produce section… How about these oranges?
A: They look a little green. I don't think they're ripe.
B: OK. Then let's get two pounds of apples and that big water-melon.
(At the check-out counter)
A: Hello. How much do we owe you?
Cashier: Twenty-four dollars and 8 cents.
A: Do you take American Express?
C: Yes, we do.

Salesclerk: Can I help you?
Customer: Yes, please. I'm looking for a shirt to go with my new suit.
S: What color are you looking for?
C: Blue.
S: What about this one? Do you like it?
C: No, it isn't the right blue.
S: Well, what about this one? It's a bit darker blue.
C: Oh yes. I like that one much better. Can I try it on?
S: Yes, of course. The fitting rooms are over there… Is the size OK?
C: No, it's a bit too big. Have you got a smaller size?
S: That's the last blue we've got, I'm afraid. But we have it in white.
C: OK, I'll take the white. There is no price tag. How much is it?
S: That'll be thirty-nine dollars with the tax. Anything else?
C: Yes. I also need running shoes.
S: Running shoes? Right over there in the sporting goods department

Day 7

3. ダイアローグ

音声を聞いて、ダイアローグの内容をはっきり理解しているか確認して下さい。

満足するまで何度でもダイアローグを声に出して読んで下さい。

ダイアローグを読む自分の声を録音してください。

ショッピング

A: ショッピングカートを持って行こう。今日はショッピングリストが長いから。
B: 分かった。乳製品から始めよう。無塩バターが1ポンド、無脂肪乳1本と、それに卵が1ケース必要だ。
A: 卵には色んなサイズがあるよ。S、M、L、XL、それにジャンボ。
B: Lサイズにしよう。セールになってるから。
A: オーケー。次は何?
B: チーズを半ポンドと、ピックルを1瓶、それにツナ缶を2つ。
A: はい、どうぞ。フルーツとか野菜はいる?
B: いるね、青果コーナーに行こう。このオレンジはどう?
A: 少し緑っぽいね。まだ熟してないと思う。
B: オーケー。じゃあ、りんごを2ポンドと、あの大きなスイカを買おう。
(レジで)
A: こんにちは。お幾らですか?
キャッシャー(Cashier): 24ドルと8セントです。
A: アメリカンエクスプレスカードで払えますか?
C: 払えますよ。

店員(Salesclerk): お手伝いしましょうか?
客 (Customer): はい、お願いします。新しいスーツに合うシャツを探しているんです。
S: どんな色をお探しですか?
C: 青です。
S: こちらのシャツはどうですか?お気に召しますか?
C: いいや、欲しい青じゃないね。
S: ええと、こちらのはどうですか?それより少し濃い青です。
C: ああ、はい。こちらの方がずっと良いですね。試着して良いですか?
S: はい、もちろんです。試着室はあちらです。。サイズはこれで良いですか?
C: いいえ、少し大き過ぎますね。これより小さいサイズはありますか?
S: 残念ですが、こちらが青では最後になります。白はあるんですけど。
C: オーケー、じゃあ白にします。値札がないです。お幾らですか?
S: 税込みで、39ドルです。他には何か必要ですか?
C: そうですね。ランニングシューズが必要です。
S: ランニングシューズですか?あちらのスポーツグッズにあります。

七日目

4. Exercise

ROLL ROLL ROLL !

Your exercise sentences are now completely irrelevant of the content of your topics or dialogues but will concentrate only on vocabulary part of your Day. Read carefully each sentence and fill in the blank spaces with missing words from your Vocabulary.

Read each sentence out loud (remember ROLL?) .

With a pencil fill in the blanks with missing words and compare your words with those used in the dialogue or topic. Do not be disappointed if you make mistakes. It is all about the effort now.

a. Who do you want to be _____ you grow up?
b. Could you _____ me a sandwich please?
c. What do you _____ better, to ride a bicycle or to rollerblade?
d. _____ do both, read and write or you ___ only read?
e. ___, I cannot write, I can only read.
f. Do you _____ if it is going to rain today?
g. Can you _____ me with you to go rollerblading?
h. This book belongs to John, so can you please give it to _____.

Day
7

4. エクササイズ

声に出して読む、声に出して読む、声に出して読んで下さい!

エクササイズの文はトピック本文やダイアローグとはもう関連がないですが、その日のボキャブラリーに焦点が置かれます。各文を注意深く読み、足りない語をボキャブラリーから空白に補ってください。

まず最初に、各文を声を出して読んで(ROLL学習法、覚えていますか?)

鉛筆を使って空白を埋め、自分の答えをダイアローグやトピックと比べて下さい。もし間違ってもがっかりしないで下さい。努力が肝心です。

a. Who do you want to be _____ you grow up?
b. Could you _____ me a sandwich please?
c. What do you _____ better, to ride a bicycle or to rollerblade?
d. _____ do both, read and write or you ___ only read?
e. ___, I cannot write, I can only read.
f. Do you _____ if it is going to rain today?
g. Can you _____ me with you to go rollerblading?
h. This book belongs to John, so can you please give it to _____.

Day 8

1. Vocabulary

Review meaning of each word on mirror translation page. Do not be concerned if you don't completely understand the meaning of each one of the words.

Listen to the Day 8 audio file and read out loud each word in the Vocabulary section repeating each word after the narrator.

Repeat the process until you are satisfied with your reading and pronunciation.

People
Into
Year
Your
Good
Some
Could
Them
See
Other

2. Topic

Please follow the same routine that I presented in Working with Topic instructions in Day 2 and Day 3.

First read through the text to gain some understanding of it by working with the mirror translation page. Don't hesitate to make marks right in the book with a pencil if you need to.

Read the entire text Out Loud as many times as it takes you to achieve flawless reading. You have to get to the stage where your reading gets easy and you don't have to pause between words and phrases.

Listen to the audio provided with this lesson and compare your pronunciation with how it is pronounced by the narrator.

八日目

1. ボキャブラリー

それぞれの単語の意味を日本語のページを見て確認して下さい。それぞれの単語の意味が完璧に分からなくても心配しないで下さい。

8日目の音声ファイルを聞いて、ボキャブラリーの部分にあるそれぞれの単語をナレーターについて声に出してリピートして下さい。

この作業をあなたの音読と発音に満足するまで続けてください。

People (人々(は))
Into (〜の中に)
Year (年)
Your (あなたの)
Good (良い)
Some (幾つかの)
Could (〜できる、可能)
Them (彼らを)
See (見る)
Other (他の)

2. トピック

2日目と、3日目のトピック部分で私が提示したやり方に則って行なってください。

最初に、ある程度理解するために、本文を日本語の部分と照らし合わせながら全て読みます。必要であれば、躊躇せずに、本に鉛筆などで印をつけてください。

本文全体を声に出して(Out Loud)何度でも完璧に読めるようになるまで繰り返し読んで下さい。読むのが簡単に感じられ、単語やフレーズで止まったりしなくても良くなる段階になるまで読んで下さい。

このレッスンの音声を聞いて、ご自分の発音をナレーターの発音と比べて下さい。

Please remember to **ROLL** from Day to Day.

My name is Nathan. I'm a security screener at Vancouver international airport. I sit at the scanner. I check people when they walk through the gate. If there is a problem, I call my supervisor. I work full time. My schedule is always different. I work different days each week. I don't have good medical benefits. I have five sick days and two weeks' vacation. I like my job at the airport. It is busy and exciting. I hope to get a promotion in the future.

Dylan is a very busy man. He is 60 years old and he has 13 jobs. He is a postman, a policeman, a fireman, a taxi driver, a boatman, an ambulance man, an accountant, a gas pump attendant, a barman, and an undertaker. Also, he and his wife, Sofia, have a shop and a small hotel.

Dylan lives and works on the Macau off the coast of China. Only 18,428 people live on Macau, but in summer 2,000 tourists come by boat every day.

Every weekday Dylan gets up at 6:00 and makes breakfast for the hotel guests. At 8:00 he drives the island's children to school. At 9:00 he collects the post from the boat and delivers it to the island's residents. He also delivers the beer to the island's only bar. Then he helps Sofia in the shop. In the evening he does the accounts.

He says: "Sofia likes being busy, too. We never go on vacation and we don't like watching television. Perhaps our life isn't very exciting, but we like it."

China Work Facts

Full-time work is between 20 and 40 hours a week.
Most people drive to work.
The minimum wage ranges from $8.00 to$10.25 an hour.
Most full-time workers receive medical benefits.
Many high school students have part-time jobs.
75% of women with children work outside the home.
Most service workers wear uniforms.
The standard retirement age is 65.

Day 8

3. Dialogue

日々、**ROLL**(声に出して読むこと)を忘れないでください。

私の名前はネィサン(Nathan)です。私はバンクーバー国際空港で安全検査官をしています。スキャナーの前に座っています。私は人々がゲートを通る際にチェックします。もし問題があれば、上司を呼びます。正社員です。私の働く時間はいつも違います。私は毎週違う曜日に働きます。あまり良い医療手当てを持っていません。5日の病気欠勤日と2週間の有給休暇があります。私はこの仕事が好きです。忙しく楽しいです。将来出世が出来るといいなと思っています。

ディラン(Dylan)はとても忙しい人です。彼は60歳で13の職を持っています。彼は郵便局職員で、警察官で、消防士で、タクシーの運転手で、船頭で、救命救急士で、会計士で、ガソリンスタンド職員で、バーの職員で、葬儀屋です。それから、彼と彼の妻ソフィア(Sophia)は一緒に店と小さなホテルをひとつずつ持っています。

ディランは中国沖のマカオに住んで働いています。マカオには18,428人しか住んでいませんが、夏には2,000人の観光客がボートで毎日来ます。

平日はいつも、ディランは6時に起きてホテルの宿泊客に朝食を作ります。8時には、島の子供たちを車で学校へ送ります。9時には郵便物をボートから集め、島の住人に配ります。また、島唯一のバーにビールを配達します。それから、店でソフィアの手伝いをします。夜には会計作業をします。

彼は言います。「ソフィアも忙しいのが好きなんだ。バケーションに行くことはないし、テレビを見るのも好きじゃない。もしかすると、私たちの生活はあまり面白くないかもしれないけど、私たちは好きです。」

中国仕事事情

フルタイムの仕事は週20〜40時間の間です。
殆どの人が車通勤です。
最低賃金は時給8ドルから10ドル25セントの間です。
殆どのフルタイム職員には医療手当てがあります。
多くの高校生がバイトをしています。
子供を持つ75%の女性が家の外で働いています。
殆どのサービス業の職員はユニフォームを着ています。
通常の定年退職年齢は65歳です。

八日目

3. ダイアローグ

Listen to the audio and make sure you understand the dialogue clearly.

Read the dialogue out loud as many times as it takes until you are satisfied with the result.

Record yourself reading the dialogue.

JOBS

Wanted:
Paris-based lifestyle magazine seeks an experienced designer to supervise layout and design team. Computer design skills are essential. Must be bilingual.

...

Interviewer: We're looking for someone with computer design skills.
Adam: I can use SesignWiz software. I also know PictureShop.
I: OK. Can you work with spreadsheets?
A: Yes, I used spreadsheets in my previous job.
I: What about your language skills? Can you speak French?
A: Yes, I can. I studied in France for three years.
I: Are you willing to travel or move to another city?
A: Yes, I love to travel and I'd be willing to relocate.
I: Why did you leave your last job?
A: I was looking for a new challenge.
I: Why do you think you're the best candidate for the job?
A: I have a lot of experience and I'm very hardworking.

Grace: Any interesting jobs listed on the Internet today?
Henry: Well, there are a lot of retail jobs – selling clothes and stuff. But you have to work Saturdays and Sundays.
G: Hmm... I hate working on weekends.
H: So do I... Oh, here's a job in sales. It's selling children's books to bookstores.
G: That sounds interesting.
H: Yeah. You need to have a driver's license. And you have to work some evenings.
G: I don't mind working evenings during the week. And I enjoy driving. So, what's the phone number?

Gavin: Where do you work, Claire?
Claire: I work for Thomas Cook Travel.
G: Oh, really? What do you do there?
C: I'm a guide. I take people on tours to South America. And what do you do?
G: I'm a student, and I have a part-time job, too.
C: Oh? Where do you work?
G: In a fast-food restaurant.

Day
8

音声を聞いて、ダイアローグの内容をはっきり理解しているか確認して下さい。

満足するまで何度でもダイアローグを声に出して読んで下さい。

ダイアローグを読む自分の声を録音してください。

仕事

求人:

パリに本拠地を置くデザインマガジンがレイアウトとデザインチームを監督する経験のあるデザイナーを探しています。コンピューターデザインのスキルは必須。バイリンガルでなければなりません。

面接官(Interviewer): 私たちはコンピューターデザインのスキルがある方を探しています。
アダム(Adam): 私は、セザインウィズ(SesignWiz)ソフトウェアを使うことが出来ます。また、ピクチャーショップ(PictureShop)も使えます。
I: 分かりました。表計算ソフトは使えますか?
A: はい、前職では表計算ソフトを使いました。
I: 言語のスキルについてはどうですか?フランス語は話せますか?
A: はい、話せます。フランスで3年間勉強しました。
I: 仕事で出張に行ったり、または、他の市に転勤になっても構いませんか?
A: はい、旅行は大好きですし、転勤も大丈夫です。
I: 前のお仕事を辞められた理由は何ですか?
A: 新しく挑戦できることを探していたものですから。
I: あなたがこの仕事に一番適した候補であるという理由を教えてください。
A: 私は経験豊富ですし、一生懸命働くからです。

グレイス(Grace): なんか良い仕事、今日はインターネットに載っていた?
ヘンリー(Henry): あー、店員の仕事は沢山あったよー服やなんかを売ったりする仕事ね。だけ ど、土日が仕事だよ。
G: ふーむ、週末に働くの嫌いなのよね。
H: 僕もだよ。ああ、ここにセールスの仕事があるよ。子供の本を本屋さんに売る仕事だよ。
G: 面白そうね。
H: そうだね。運転免許が必要だよ。それから、時々夜も働かないといけないよ。
G: 平日の夜に働くのは構わないわ。それに運転好きだし。電話番号は?

ギャビン (Gavin): クレア、君どこで働いているの?
クレア (Claire): トーマスクックトラベルで働いているわ。
G: え、本当?そこで何をしているの?
C: ガイドよ。南アメリカのツアーにお客さんを連れて行くの。あなたは何しているの?
G: 学生だよ、それからバイトもしているよ。
C: そうなの?どこで働いているの?
G: ファーストフード店で働いているよ。

八日目

4. Exercise

Don't forget ROLL!

Your exercise sentences are now completely irrelevant of the content of your topics or dialogues but will concentrate only on vocabulary part of your Day. Read carefully each sentence and fill in the blank spaces with missing words from your Vocabulary.

Read each sentence out loud (remember ROLL?) .

With a pencil fill in the blanks with missing words and compare your words with those used in the dialogue or topic.

a. Many _____ visit Italy every year.

b. If you want to try this key you need to insert it _____ the lock and try turning.

c. I take vacations every _____.

d. _____ class is almost started, you need to hurry up or you will be late.

e. This is a very _____ book, I liked it very much.

f. _____ people prefer skiing to skating.

g. _____ you please help me to understand this sentence.

h. Can you please _____ if you have time to help me with my study?

4. エクササイズ

ROLL(声に出して読む事)する事を忘れないでください！

エクササイズの文はトピック本文やダイアローグとはもう関連がないですが、その日のボキャブラリーに焦点が置かれます。各文を注意深く読み、足りない語をボキャブラリーから空白に補ってください。

まず最初に、各文を声を出して読んで(ROLL学習法、覚えていますか？)

鉛筆を使って空白を埋め、自分の答えをダイアローグやトピックと比べて下さい。

a. Many _____ visit Italy every year.
b. If you want to try this key you need to insert it _____ the lock and try turning.
c. I take vacations every _____.
d. _____ class is almost started, you need to hurry up or you will be late.
e. This is a very _____ book, I liked it very much.
f. _____ people prefer skiing to skating.
g. _____ you please help me to understand this sentence.
h. Can you please _____ if you have time to help me with my study?

八日目

Day 9

1. Vocabulary

Review meaning of each word on mirror translation page. Do not be concerned if you don't completely understand the meaning of each one of the words.

Listen to the Day 9 audio file and read out loud each word in the Vocabulary section repeating each word after the narrator.

Repeat the process until you are satisfied with your reading and pronunciation.

Than
Then
Now
Look
Only
Come
Its
Over
Think
Also

2. Topic

Please follow the same routine that I presented in Working with Topic instructions in Day 2 and Day 3.

First read through the text to gain some understanding of it by working with the mirror translation page. Don't hesitate to make marks right in the book with a pencil if you need to.

Read the entire text Out Loud as many times as it takes you to achieve flawless reading. You have to get to the stage where your reading gets easy and you don't have to pause between words and phrases.

Listen to the audio provided with this lesson and compare your pronunciation with how it is pronounced by the narrator.

九日目

1. ボキャブラリー

それぞれの単語の意味を日本語のページを見て確認して下さい。それぞれの単語の意味が完璧に分からなくても心配しないで下さい。

9日目の音声ファイルを聞いて、ボキャブラリーの部分にあるそれぞれの単語をナレーターについて声に出してリピートして下さい。

この作業をあなたの音読と発音に満足するまで続けてください。

Than (〜より)
Then (そして)
Now (今)
Look (見る)
Only (〜だけ)
Come (来る)
Its (それの)
Over (終わり、〜以上)
Think (考える、思う)
Also (また、〜もまた)

2. トピック

2日目と、3日目のトピック部分で私が提示したやり方に則って行なってください。

最初に、ある程度理解するために、本文を日本語の部分と照らし合わせながら全て読みます。必要であれば、躊躇せずに、本に鉛筆などで印をつけてください。

本文全体を声に出して(Out Loud)何度でも完璧に読めるようになるまで繰り返し読んで下さい。読むのが簡単に感じられ、単語やフレーズで止まったりしなくても良くなる段階になるまで読んで下さい。

このレッスンの音声を聞いて、ご自分の発音をナレーターの発音と比べて下さい。

Please remember to **ROLL** from Day to Day.

Letter to the Editor

Dear Editor,
I'm sick and tired of the traffic in this city! It is so bad that I can never get anywhere on time. There are too many cars on the road, and most of them have only one person in them.

Another problem is the buses. They are so old and slow that nobody wants to take them. They are noisy and dirty. You can't even see out of the windows!

Also, the taxi drivers are rude. They never know where they are going, and they take a long time to get places. Taxis are expensive, too. And they are often late when you call them over the phone. And the subway is just too crowded and dangerous. What are we going to do?

Jordan

Aaron flies to Detroit

Aaron bought a return airline ticket to Detroit. He arrived at the airport and checked in for the flight two hours before the departure. He took his laptop as hand baggage and checked in a suitcase with his clothes. The man at the check-in desk gave him a boarding pass and told him to go to Gate 15. Soon Aaron boarded the plane, sat down and put on his seat belt. The plane took off on time. It was a direct flight, so Aaron didn't have to worry about missing his connection. Two hours later the plane landed in Detroit. Aaron collected his baggage and met his friends.

Getting a Driver's License

When I came to this country three years ago, I didn't know how to drive. Public transportation wasn't good, so I had to go to work by car. My brother taught me how to drive, so I didn't need to take lessons at the driving school. Every weekend my brother took me to the high school parking lot. I practiced going straight, backing up, turning, stopping and parking. I was also memorizing the traffic rules for a written test.

Day 9

After six weeks, I passed the written test. Then I took the driving test, but I made a lot of mistakes. I forgot to signal when I turned, I didn't stop at a stop sign, and I didn't park correctly. I failed the test. After that I practiced more, both in my neighborhood and downtown. Four weeks later I passed the driving test and got a driver's license.

日々、**ROLL(声に出して読む事)**をする事を忘れないでください。

編集者への手紙

親愛なる編集者様
私はこの市の交通に飽き飽きしています！本当に交通が悪くて、何処にも決して時間通りには着けません。道路には車が多過ぎるし、しかも殆どの車は１人しか乗っていません。

他の問題は、バスです。バスは古いし、遅くて誰も乗りたいと思いません。うるさいし汚いです。(汚くて)窓から外を見ることも出来ません。

それから、タクシーの運転手は失礼です。いつも彼らは目的地にどう行ったらいいか分からないので、着くまでに長い時間がかかります。それにタクシーは高いです。それに、電話でタクシーを呼ぶと大抵来るのが遅いです。それから、地下鉄は混んでいて危険です。どうしたら良いんでしょう？

ジョーダン(Jordan)

アーロン(Aaron)、デトロイトへ飛ぶ

アーロンは、デトロイトまでの往復航空券を買いました。出発の２時間前には空港に着いてチェックインを済ませました。ラップトップを機内持ち込みにし、洋服の入ったスーツケースをチェックインしました。チェックインデスクの係員はアーロンに搭乗券を渡し、15番ゲートに行ってくださいと言いました。すぐにアーロンは飛行機に乗り込み、席について、シートベルトを締めました。飛行機は時間通りに飛び立ちました。直行便なので、アーロンは乗り継ぎに遅れる心配をしなくて良いです。２時間後、飛行機はデトロイトに着陸しました。アーロンは荷物を引き取って、友達に会いました。

運転免許取得

この国に３年前にやって来た時には、私は運転の仕方を知りませんでした。公共交通機関は良くなかったので、車通勤せざるを得ませんでした。兄が運転の仕方を教えてくれたので、教習所で習う必要がありませんでした。毎週末、兄は私を高校の駐車場に連れて行ってくれました。まっすぐ進んだり、後ろに下がったり、曲がったり、止まったり、駐車したりという練習をしました。また、交通ルールを覚えてテストに備えました。

６週間後には、私は筆記試験をパスしました。それから、私は実技試験を受けました、だけど、沢山間違いをしました。曲がるときにウィンカーを忘れたり、止まれのサインで止まらなかったり、きちんと駐車できませんでした。試験には落ちました。その後、私は近所と街中で更に練習をしました。４週間後、実技試験に合格し、運転免許を取りました。

九日日

3. Dialogue

Listen to the audio and make sure you understand the dialogue clearly.

Read the dialogue out loud as many times as it takes until you are satisfied with the result.

Record yourself reading the dialogue.

Transportation, Directions

A: Shall we take a cab or a bus to the meeting?
B: We'd better take a bus. It's almost impossible to find a taxi during rush hour.
A: Isn't that a bus stop over there?
B: Yes... Oh, oh! There's a bus now. We'll have to run to catch it.
A: OK... Oh, no! We just missed it.
B: Never mind. There'll be another one in ten minutes.

Passenger: Does this bus go to Central Park?
Bus Driver: No, you have to transfer to another bus.
P: Which bus do I need?
BD: You need bus 138. Get off two stops after this one and take bus 138 from there.

A: Excuse me. Is there a bank near here?
B: Yes, there is one next to Harrods Department Store.
A: How do I get there?
B: Go straight ahead two blocks. It's on the right.
A: Thanks a lot.

A: Excuse me. Could you tell me which way Chapters bookstore is?
B: Yes, it's that way. Turn right at the traffic lights, then take the second turn to the left. You can't miss it. It's on the corner across from the coffee shop.
A: Is it far?
B: No, it's only about five minutes' walk.
A: Thanks. I'm new here, so I really don't know my way around yet.
B: Oh, I know how you feel.
A: Is there a post office nearby?
B: Yes, there is one on Commercial Street, next to the police station.
A: I see... And where is the police station?
B: It's between the insurance agency and the movie theater.
A: And where is Commercial Street?
B: Commercial Street is around the corner from this building.
A: Oh, thank you.

Day 9

3. ダイアローグ

音声を聞いて、ダイアローグの内容をはっきり理解しているか確認して下さい。

満足するまで何度でもダイアローグを声に出して読んで下さい。

ダイアローグを読む自分の声を録音してください。

交通機関・道順

A: ミーティングに行くのに、タクシーに乗る?それともバスにする?
B: バスに乗った方がいいね。ラッシュアワーにタクシーを拾うのは殆ど不可能に近いから。
A: あそこにあるの、バス停じゃない?
B: そうだね、、、ゲッ、もうバスが来たよ。走らないと間に合わない。
A: オーケー、あーだめだ!丁度乗り損ねたよ。
B: 気にするなよ。次のが10分後に来るから。

乗客(Passenger) : このバス、セントラルパークに行きますか?
バスの運転手(Bus Driver): いいえ、他のバスに乗り換えないといけません。
P: どのバスですか?
B: 138番のバスですね。この後2番目のバス停で降りて、138番のバスにそこで乗ってください。

A: すみません。この近くに銀行はありますか?
B: はい、ハロッズデパートの隣にありますよ。
A: どうやって行ったらいいですか?
B: ここをまっすぐ前方に2ブロック行って下さい。そしたら右側にあります。
A: 本当にありがとう。

A: すみません。チャプターズの本屋はどっち教えてくれませんか?
B: はい、あっちです。信号で右に曲がって、2番目の道を左に曲がります。すぐ分かりますよ。コーヒーショップの向かいの角です。
A: 遠いですか?
B: いいえ、5分ほど歩けば着きますよ。
A: ありがとう。最近越してきたので、まだあまりよく知らないんです。
B: 分かるわ。
A: 近くに郵便局はありますか?
B: はい、コマーシャルストリートにひとつあって、警察署の隣です。
A: そうなんですね、、、警察署は何処ですか?
B: 警察署は、保険屋と映画館の間にあります。
A: コマーシャルストリートは何処ですか?
B: コマーシャルストリートは、このビルを曲がったところにあります。
A: ありがとうございます。

4. Exercise

Keep ROLL-ing!

Your exercise sentences are now completely irrelevant to the content of your topics or dialogues but will concentrate only on vocabulary part of your Day. Read carefully each sentence and fill the blanks with missing words from your Vocabulary.

Read each sentence out loud (remember ROLL?) .

With a pencil fill in the blanks with missing words and compare your words with those used in the dialogue or topic.

a. I have had enough of studying English, I would like to take some rest ____.

b. Please ____ inside this treasure box, there are beautiful gold coins inside.

c. Would you like to ____ to my birthday party?

d. You lose, the game is ____.

e. I ____ you should get some more studying done instead of playing games.

f. I would like a coffee and a sandwich. I would ____ like a fruit salad with that.

g. I have two rooms in my house. For myself ____ it is more then enough.

4.エクササイズ

ROLL (声に出して読む)し続けてください!

エクササイズの文はトピック本文やダイアローグとはもう関連がないですが、その日のボキャブラリーに焦点が置かれます。各文を注意深く読み、足りない語をボキャブラリーから空白に補ってください。

まず最初に、各文を声を出して読んで(ROLL学習法、覚えていますか?)

鉛筆を使って空白を埋め、自分の答えをダイアローグやトピックと比べて下さい。

a. I have had enough of studying English, I would like to take some rest _____.

b. Please _____ inside this treasure box, there are beautiful gold coins inside.

c. Would you like to _____ to my birthday party?

d. You lose, the game is _____.

e. I _____ you should get some more studying done instead of playing games.

f. I would like a coffee and a sandwich. I would _____ like a fruit salad with that.

g. I have two rooms in my house. For myself _____ it is more then enough.

九日目

Day 10

1. Vocabulary

Review meaning of each word on mirror translation page. Do not be concerned if you don't completely understand the meaning of each one of the words.

Listen to the Day 10 audio file and read out loud each word in the Vocabulary section repeating each word after the narrator.

Repeat the process until you are satisfied with your reading and pronunciation.

Back
After
Use
Two
How
Our
Work
First
Well
Way

2. Topic

Please follow the same routine that I presented in Working with Topic instructions in Day 2 and Day 3.

First read through the text to gain some understanding of it by working with the mirror translation page. Don't hesitate to make marks right in the book with a pencil if you need to.

Read the entire text Out Loud as many times as it takes you to achieve flawless reading. You have to get to the stage where your reading gets easy and you don't have to pause between words and phrases.

Listen to the audio provided with this lesson and compare your pronunciation with how it is pronounced by the narrator.

十日目

1. ボキャブラリー

それぞれの単語の意味を日本語のページを見て確認して下さい。それぞれの単語の意味が完璧に分からなくても心配しないで下さい。

10日目の音声ファイルを聞いて、ボキャブラリーの部分にあるそれぞれの単語をナレーターについて声に出してリピートして下さい。

この作業をあなたの音読と発音に満足するまで続けてください。

Back (戻って、後ろ、背中)
After (〜の後)
Use (使う)
Two (ふたつ)
How (どうやって、どう)
Our (私たちの)
Work (働く、仕事)
First (最初)
Well (上手に)
Way (方法、道)

2. トピック

2日目と、3日目のトピック部分で私が提示したやり方に則って行なってください。

最初に、ある程度理解するために、本文を日本語の部分と照らし合わせながら全て読みます。必要であれば、躊躇せずに、本に鉛筆などで印をつけてください。

本文全体を声に出して(Out Loud)何度でも完璧に読めるようになるまで繰り返し読んで下さい。読むのが簡単に感じられ、単語やフレーズで止まったりしなくても良くなる段階になるまで読んで下さい。

このレッスンの音声を聞いて、ご自分の発音をナレーターの発音と比べて下さい。

Please remember to **ROLL** from Day to Day.

Come to Killington!

Skiing: Killington has one of the largest ski areas in the world. Enjoy 180 lifts and over 300 km of perfect snow!

Accommodations: Bear Inn is a modern hotel with relaxing atmosphere and fine dining. It has a swimming pool, a sauna, free cable and wireless Internet. Luxurious rooms feature Jacuzzis and fireplaces. And it's only 5 minutes from the nearest ski lift.

Price includes: All ski equipment, lift tickets, and daily two-hour lessons.

Nightlife: There are bars and clubs open till late, and fantastic restaurants for all tastes.

Additional activities: Antique shopping, cross-country skiing, sledding, ice-skating.

Rates: Single room – from $1,200 a week, double room – from $1,600 a week.

Vacation Postcards

Dear Homer,

Alaska is terrific! I was just on a trip in the Arctic National Wildlife Refuge. There were six people on the trip. We hiked for ten days. Then we took rafts to the Arctic Ocean. I saw a lot of wildlife. Now I'm going to Anchorage. See you in three weeks!

Love, Gloria

Hi, Julia!

My Hawaiian vacation just ended, and I am very relaxed! I spent my whole vacation at a spa in Koloa, Kauai. Every day for a week I exercised, did yoga, meditated, and ate vegetarian food. I also went swimming and snorkeling. I feel fantastic!

Day
10

Love, Charles

日々、**ROLL(声に出して読む事)**を忘れないでください。

キリングトン(Killington)へお越しください!

スキー:キリングトンには世界でも有数の大きなスキー場があります。180機のリフトと、300km以上のパーフェクトな雪をお楽しみください。

宿泊:ベア・イン(Bear Inn)は、近代的なホテルで、リラックスできる雰囲気とお洒落な料理があります。スイミングプールと、サウナ、テレビとワイヤレスインターネットを完備しています。高級感のある部屋には、ジャグジーと暖炉があります。それに一番近いスキーのリフトまではたったの5分です。

値段に含まれるもの:スキー用品全て、リフトのチケット、そして、毎日2時間のレッスン。

ナイトライフ: バーやクラブは遅くまで開いており、どんな好みにも合う素晴らしいレストランがあります。

その他のアクティビティ:アンティーク(骨董品)ショッピング、クロスカントリースキー、そり滑り、スケート。

料金: シングルルーム-週1200ドルから。ダブルルーム-週1600ドルから。

旅行絵葉書

親愛なるホーマーさんへ

アラスカは素晴らしいです!丁度、北極国家野生動物保護の旅行に参加し終えたところです。旅行には6人参加しました。10日間ハイキングしました。それから、北極海へゴムボートで行きました。野生動物を沢山見ました。これから、アンカレッジに行きます。3週間後に会いましょう!

愛を込めて、グロリア(Gloria)

こんにちは、ジュリア(Julia)!

ハワイでの休暇がちょうど終わって、ゆっくりしている所です。カウアイ島のコロアの温泉場でずっと過ごしました。1週間毎日運動して、ヨガ、瞑想し、それから食べ物はベジタリアンでした。泳ぎに行ったり、シュノーケリングにも行きました。本当にいい気分だよ。

愛を込めて、チャールズ(Charles)

十日

Julian,

I'm on vacation in Rome with my girlfriend. We're staying in a small hotel near the Coliseum. During the day we walk around the city and take a lot of photos. At night we go to restaurants and have fantastic pasta and red wine. We're having a great time. Rome is full of history and has a special atmosphere. We only have two problems: it is very hot, and it is very difficult to cross the road.

Take care, Brandon

3. Dialogue

Listen to the audio and make sure you understand the dialogue clearly.

Read the dialogue out loud as many times as it takes until you are satisfied with the result.

Record yourself reading the dialogue.

Vacations, Weather

Austin: Hello, Robert? It's Austin. I'm calling from Los Angeles.
Robert: Austin! Hi! How is your vacation going?
A: Great! Los Angeles is beautiful!
R: How is the weather? I'll bet it's really nice.
A: Yeah, sunny and very hot. I think it's about 35 degrees.
R: Wow, that is hot! What did you do today?
A: We went surfing this morning and scuba diving after lunch. How is the weather in Toronto?
R: It's quite cold. And it's raining heavily.
A: And what is the weather forecast for tomorrow? We are returning tomorrow.
R: It's supposed to be warm and sunny.

A: I'm so excited! We have two weeks off! What are you going to do?
B: I'm not sure. I guess I'll just stay home. Maybe I'll redecorate my living room or do some gardening. What about you? Any plans?
A: Well, my parents have rented a cottage on an island. I'm going to take long walks along the beach every day and do lots of swimming.
B: Sounds great!
A: Say, why don't you come with us? We have plenty of room.
B: Do you mean it? I'd love to!

Day
10

110

ジュリアン(Julian)

今、彼女と休暇でローマに来ているんだ。コロシアムの近くの小さなホテルに滞在しているよ。日中は市内を歩き回って沢山写真を撮っています。夜にはレストランに行って、美味しいパスタと赤ワインを頂いているよ。本当に楽しい時を過ごしているよ。ローマには本当に沢山の歴史があって、特別な雰囲気があるよ。問題は2つだけ－とっても暑い事と、道路を渡るのがとても大変だって事。

じゃあね、ブランドン(Brandon)

3. ダイアローグ

音声を聞いて、ダイアローグの内容をはっきり理解しているか確認して下さい。

満足するまで何度でもダイアローグを声に出して読んで下さい。

ダイアローグを読む自分の声を録音してください。

休暇・天気

オースティン(Austin): もしもし、ロバート？オースティンです。ロサンゼルスからかけています。
ロバート(Robert): オースティン！こんにちは！休暇はどうですか？
A: とても良いよ！ロサンゼルスは美しいよ！
R: 天気はどうだい？とても良いだろうと想像するけど。
A: そうだね、晴れでとても暑いよ。35度くらいじゃないかなあ。
R: ええーっ、それは暑いね。今日は何したの？
A: 僕たちは今朝、サーフィンに行って、お昼の後はスキューバダイビングをしたよ。トロントの天気はどうだい？
R: かなり寒いよ。それに雨も激しく降っているよ。
A: 明日の天気予報はどうなっている？明日帰るんだ。
R: 暖かくて晴れるそうだよ。

A: 本当にワクワクしているよ。2週間の休みだ！君は何をするの？
B: まだ分かんないな。多分家にいると思うよ。リビングを模様替えするか、ガーデニングしようかな。君は？何か予定ある？
A: うーん、両親が島に別荘を借りたんだ。毎日海岸沿いで長い散歩をして、いっぱい泳ぐよ。
B: わーいいなあ！
A: ねえ、君も一緒に来たら？スペースは十分にあるよ。
B: 本当にいいの？喜んで！

111

Hotel Operator: Hilton Hotel. How can I help you?

Andy: I'd like to make a reservation for August 20th through the 22nd, please.

HO: For how many people?

A: Just for myself. And could I have a non-smoking room, please?

HO: Just a moment, please... Yes, I have a single non-smoking room available. That room is $125 a night. The price includes a continental breakfast.

A: That will be fine. Can I put that on my credit card?

HO: Yes, of course.

A: And what is the check-out time?

HO: It's 11 am.

A: Thank you.

4. Exercise

ROLL !

Your exercise sentences are now completely irrelevant to the content of your topics or dialogues but will concentrate only on vocabulary part of your Day. Read carefully each sentence and fill the blanks with missing words from your Vocabulary.

Read each sentence out loud (remember ROLL?) .

With a pencil fill in the blanks with missing words and compare your words with those used in the dialogue or topic.

a. I feel that I am starting to forget what I learned, I need to go _____ to school.

b. I watch TV only _____ I have my homework done.

c. Some people don't even know how to _____ chopsticks.

d. One, _____, three, four, five.

e. I know _____ to read.

f. We all love _____ house.

g. I have to go to _____ every morning.

h. I need to read the instructions _____ and then try to follow them.

i. My father thinks that I am doing very _____ at my studying.

j. Can you please tell me if this is the right way to the library?

Day

10

Hotel Operator: ヒルトンホテルです。ご用件をお伺いします。
Andy: 8月20日〜22日まで予約したいんですが。
HO: 何名様ですか?
A: 私だけです。禁煙の部屋にして頂けませんか?
HO: 少しお待ちください、、、はい、シングルの禁煙室が空いています。その部屋は1泊125ドルです。料金には軽い朝食も含まれています。
A: 大丈夫です。クレジットカードで払えますか?
HO: はい、もちろんです。
A: チェックアウトの時間は何時ですか?
HO: 11時です。
A: ありがとうございます。

4. エクササイズ

ROLL (声に出して読んで下さい)!

エクササイズの文はトピック本文やダイアローグとはもう関連がないですが、その日のボキャブラリーに焦点が置かれます。各文を注意深く読み、足りない語をボキャブラリーから空白に補ってください。

まず最初に、各文を声を出して読んで(ROLL学習法、覚えていますか?)

鉛筆を使って空白を埋め、自分の答えをダイアローグやトピックと比べて下さい。

a. I feel that I am starting to forget what I learned, I need to go _____ to school.
b. I watch TV only _____ I have my homework done.
c. Some people don't even know how to _____ chopsticks.
d. One, _____, three, four, five.
e. I know _____ to read.
f. We all love _____ house.
g. I have to go to _____ every morning.
h. I need to read the instructions _____ and then try to follow them.
i. My father thinks that I am doing very _____ at my studying.
j. Can you please tell me if this is the right way to the library?

十日目

113

Bonus Day

1. Vocabulary

Review meaning of each word on mirror translation page. Do not be concerned if you don't completely understand the meaning of each one of the words.

Listen to the Bonus Day audio file and read out loud each word in the Vocabulary section repeating each word after the narrator.

Repeat the process until you are satisfied with your reading and pronunciation.

Even
New
Want
Because
Any
These
Give
Day
Most
Us

2. Topic

Please follow the same routine that I presented in Working with Topic instructions in Day 2 and Day 3.

First read through the text to gain some understanding of it by working with the mirror translation page. Don't hesitate to make marks right in the book with a pencil if you need to.

Read the entire text Out Loud as many times as it takes you to achieve flawless reading. You have to get to the stage where your reading gets easy and you don't have to pause between words and phrases.

Listen to the audio provided with this lesson and compare your pronunciation with how it is pronounced by the narrator.

114

ボーナス日

1.ボキャブラリー

それぞれの単語の意味を日本語のページを見て確認して下さい。それぞれの単語の意味が完璧に分からなくても心配しないで下さい。

音声ファイルを聞いて、ボキャブラリーの部分にあるそれぞれの単語をナレーターについて声に出してリピートして下さい。

この作業をあなたの音読と発音に満足するまで続けてください。

Even (〜さえ)
New (新しい)
Want (欲しい)
Because (〜だから)
Any (どれか、どれも)
These (これらは、これらの)
Give (あげる)
Day (日)
Most (殆ど(の))
Us (私たち(に))

2.トピック

2日目と、3日目のトピック部分で私が提示したやり方に則って行なってください。

最初に、ある程度理解するために、本文を日本語の部分と照らし合わせながら全て読みます。必要であれば、躊躇せずに、本に鉛筆などで印をつけてください。

本文全体を声に出して(Out Loud)何度でも完璧に読めるようになるまで繰り返し読んで下さい。読むのが簡単に感じられ、単語やフレーズで止まったりしなくても良くなる段階になるまで読んで下さい。

このレッスンの音声を聞いて、ご自分の発音をナレーターの発音と比べて下さい。

Please remember to **ROLL** from Day to Day.

Ten Ways to Improve Your Health

Believe it or not, you can greatly improve your health in these ten simple ways:
(1) Eat breakfast – Breakfast gives you energy for the morning.
(2) Go for a walk – Walking is good exercise, and exercise is necessary for good health.
(3) Floss your teeth – Don't just brush them. Flossing keeps your gums healthy.
(4) Drink eight cups of water every day – Water helps your body in many ways.
(5) Stretch for five minutes – Stretching is important for your muscles.
(6) Do something to challenge your brain – For example, do a crossword puzzle or read a new book.
(7) Moisturize your skin and use sunscreen.
(8) Get enough calcium – Your bones need it. Yogurt and milk have calcium.
(9) Take a "time-out" – Break for 20 minutes and do something different. For example, get up and walk. Or sit down and listen to music.
(10) Wear a seat belt – Every year seat belts save thousands of lives.

We all know that exercise is good for health. So on January 1st we often start the New Year with a decision to go to the gym three times a week. But what happens? The first week we go three times, the second week we go twice, and the third week we stop going. The same thing happens with diets.

Kevin, a personal trainer, says this is because winter is the wrong season to start new exercise routines and diets. "In the winter, the days are short, and dark, and cold. Our bodies want food and sleep, not diets and exercise." His advice is to make small changes. "Try to cut out chocolate and cakes for three days a week. Go for short walks during the day, when it's light. But when March comes and spring begins, that's the time to get up at 7:00, have a fruit juice for breakfast, and go jogging!"

3. Dialogue

Listen to the audio and make sure you understand the dialogue clearly.

Read the dialogue out loud as many times as it takes until you are satisfied with the result.

Record yourself reading the dialogue.

日々、**ROLLする事(声に出して読む事)**を忘れないでください。

健康を増進する10の方法

信じるか信じないかはその人次第ですが、これらの簡単な10の方法で大きく健康増進することが出来ます。

(1)朝食を食べる－朝食は午前中に必要なエネルギーを与えてくれます。

(2)散歩に行く－歩く事は良い運動です、そして運動は健康には欠かせません。

(3)歯をフロスする－みがくだけではいけません。フロスする事によって歯茎の健康が保たれます。

(4)毎日水を8杯飲む－水はいろんな意味で体に役立ちます。

(5)5分間ストレッチする－ストレッチする事は筋肉にとって重要です。

(6)脳にチャレンジするような事をする－例えば、クロスワードパズルをしたり、新しい本を読む等。

(7)肌に保湿をして、日焼け止めを塗る。

(8)十分なカルシウムを摂る－骨に必要です。ヨーグルトやミルクにはカルシウムが入っています。

(9)タイムアウトをとる－20分休憩して、何か違う事をしてください。例えば、椅子から起き上がって歩いてください。または、座って音楽を聴いてください。

(10)シートベルトを締める－毎年シートベルトは何千人もの命を救っています。

私たちは皆、運動が健康に良いと知っています。なので、1月1日には私たちは週に3回ジムに行くぞなどという新年の決意をしたりします。だけど、その後何が起こりますか？最初の週は3回行きます、2週目は2回、3週目には行くのをやめてしまいます。同じ事がダイエットにも言えます。

パーソナルトレーナーのケビンは冬という季節に新しい運動やダイエットといった習慣を始めるのが間違っていると言います。「冬は日が短くて、暗くて寒いです。私たちの体は食べ物と睡眠を欲しがり、ダイエットや運動は欲しがっていません。」彼のアドバイスは小さな変化を持つことだといいます。「週に3回はチョコレートやケーキを絶つようにしてください。日中の明るい時に短い散歩に出てください。然し、3月がやってきて春が始まれば、朝7時に起きて果物のジュースを朝食にし、ジョギングに出かけてください。」

3. ダイアローグ

音声を聞いて、ダイアローグの内容をはっきり理解しているか確認して下さい。

満足するまで何度でもダイアローグを声に出して読んで下さい。

ダイアローグを読む自分の声を録音してください。

117

A: Are you OK? You look terrible.
B: I don't feel well.
A: What's the matter?
B: I have a terrible headache.
A: Did you take some aspirin?
B: Yes, I did, but it's not working. I also have a fever, and my throat is burning.
A: Oh, then it must be the flu. Have you seen the doctor yet?
B: I hate doctors. I prefer taking some medicine and staying in bed for a couple of days.
A: I hope you feel better soon. By the way, have you heard about Mrs. Simpson?
B: No. What about her?
A: She had such a bad case of the flu that they had to take her to the hospital.
B: Oh, I'm sorry to hear that!

Pharmacist: Good afternoon. Can I help you?
A: Yes. Can you make up this prescription, please?
P: Certainly. Would you like to wait? It'll be ready in 15 minutes.
A: Sure, I'll wait.
P: Anything else I can do for you?
A: Yes. I've got a bad stomach ache.
P: Well, try this medicine. Take two tablets with water every three hours.
A: All right. Thank you.

A: You're in great shape. Do you work out at a gym?
B: Yeah, I do. I guess I'm a real fitness freak.
A: So, how often do you work out?
B: Well, I do aerobics three days a week after work. And I do Pilates twice a week. Besides, I jog every morning. How about you?
A: I prefer outdoor sports, such as cycling, hiking and skiing. I also play tennis.
B: Yes, I like tennis, too. Do you want to play sometime?

Lucy cut her finger last week. It was bleeding a lot. She went to the emergency room, where she filled out a medical form and spoke with the screening nurse. Then she waited to see the doctor. The doctor examined her finger and said it was a bad cut. Lucy needed a tetanus shot. She needed about ten stitches, too. The doctor bandaged her finger to keep it clean. He told Lucy to come back one week later to have the stitches removed.

A: 大丈夫？顔色がとても悪いけど。
B: 気分が良くないんだ。
A: どうしたの？
B: ひどい頭痛がしてね。
A: 頭痛薬飲んだ？
B: うん、飲んだよ、だけど効いてないんだ。熱もあるし、喉が焼けるように痛いよ。
A: じゃあ、インフルエンザじゃないかな？お医者さんには診てもらった？
B: 医者は嫌いなんだ。薬を飲んで２−３日家で寝ていたほうが良いよ。
A: 早く良くなるといいけど。ところで、シンプソンさんの事聞いた？
B: いいえ。何のこと？
A: 彼女、悪いインフルエンザにかかってね、病院に運ばれたんだ。
B: ええっ、それは大変だったね。

薬剤師（Pharmacist）: こんにちは。何か御用ですか？
A: はい。この処方箋の薬を出してもらえませんか？
P: 分かりました。お待ちになりますか？１５分ほどで出来ますが。
A: そうですね、待ちます。
P: 他に何かありましたか？
A: ええ。ひどい腹痛があるんです。
P: ええと、この薬を試してみてください。３時間毎に２つタブレットを水と一緒に飲んでください。
A: 分かりました。ありがとうございます。

A: とても引き締まって健康そうですね。ジムで運動してるのですか？
B: ええ、しています。フィットネスおたくだと思います。
A: そうすると、どのくらい頻繁に運動するのですか？
B: えーと、仕事の後週に３回エアロビをします。それから、ピラーティスを週に２回します。その他に、毎朝ジョギングに行きます。あなたは？
A: サイクリングやハイキング、それにスキーといったアウトドアのスポーツの方が好きですね。テニスもします。
B: 私もテニスが好きです。いつか一緒にやりませんか？

ルーシー(Lucy)は、先週指を切ってしまいました。血が沢山出ていました。彼女は、緊急治療室に行って、用紙に記入をして、看護婦と話をしました。その後、医者が来るのを待ちました。医者が診て、ひどい切り傷だねと言いました。ルーシーは破傷風の予防接種が必要でした。また、１０針縫いました。医者は傷口を綺麗に保てるように、彼女の指に包帯を巻きました。医者はルーシーに１週間後に抜糸をするのでまた来てくださいと伝えました。
11

4. Exercise

Read each sentence out loud (remember ROLL?).

With a pencil fill in the blanks with missing words and compare your words with those used in the dialogue or topic.

a. Jose is an expert but _____ he doesn't know how to fix this.

b. This is my _____ computer. It works much better than the old one.

c. I am thirsty. I _____ to have a glass of water.

d. I am getting better at learning English _____ I work hard.

e. _____ shoes are very nice, I am wearing them right now.

f. I would like to _____ this coat to a homeless person. It is cold outside.

g. I learn English taking one _____ at the time.

h. The bus is full of people _____ of them are going to the soccer game.

i. This is the map of the city. It will help _____ to find the way around.

4. エクササイズ

まず最初に、各文を声を出して読んで(ROLL学習法、覚えていますか?)

鉛筆を使って空白を埋め、自分の答えをダイアローグやトピックと比べて下さい。

a. Jose is an expert but _____ he doesn't know how to fix this.
b. This is my _____ computer. It works much better than the old one.
c. I am thirsty. I _____ to have a glass of water.
d. I am getting better at learning English _____ I work hard.
e. _____ shoes are very nice, I am wearing them right now.
f. I would like to _____ this coat to a homeless person. It is cold outside.
g. I learn English taking one _____ at the time.
h. The bus is full of people _____ of them are going to the soccer game.
i. This is the map of the city. It will help _____ to find the way around.

Where do I go from here

Your Achievement

If you reading this then I believe you now have something to brag about. You completed the entire book and I am sure have a good reason to be satisfied and proud of your achievement. You now should be able to engage in a conversation with anyone who speaks English. Congratulations!

Most Important Is A Real Life Communication

Going forward you will always be improving your English as long as you keep using it. Please remember that the most important part of learning new language is actual communication with real people. If you really want your English to keep improving take every possible chance to use it.

Don't be shy and talk to people anywhere you can. In a bookstore, when you pick up a newspaper, in a community center. Shyness is your enemy. Being shy you may miss on so many interesting events in life, so if you are shy, try to do the best you can to fight it and overcome it as much as you can. Don't miss on any opportunity to talk to people.

English Language Websites

You can now browse English language websites. To make sure the process is enjoyable, keep it fun. Search information online about something that you really like.

There is a wealth of language learning resources online that you can browse through and find some useful tips on how to keep improving your English. Here are a few websites you could start with:

www.talkenglish.com
www.englishclub.com
www.livemocha.com

I would like to extend my warmest gratitude and appreciation for trusting me and taking on this book as your learning aid. I hope that you had a great time and enjoyable experience.

I truly believe that now, being able to speak English will make a huge difference in your life.

その後の指

あなたの達成したもの

も しあなたがこれを読んでいるのであれば、あなたは今、自慢していいものが あると信じます。あなたはこの本を最後までやり、きっとご自分の達成の成 果に満足し誇りに思う尤もな理由をお持ちだと思います。英語を話すどんな人と も会話する事が出来る筈です。おめでとうございます！

一番大切なのは、実生活のコミュニケーション

英語を使い続ける限り、あなたの英語は常に上達します。新しい言語を学ぶ上で 一番大切な事は、実在する人々との現実のコミュニケーションだと覚えておいてく ださい。本当に英語を上達し続けたいなら、英語を使うどんな機会も逃さない事 です。

恥ずかしがらずに、出来るところ何処ででも人に話しかけてください。本屋で、新 聞を買うとき、コミュニティセンターで。恥ずかしがる事はあなたの敵です。恥ずか しがる事で、沢山ある興味深い出来事を逃してしまうかもしれません、ですから、 もしあなたが恥かしがり屋であれば、それと戦って、出来る限り克服してください。 人に話しかけるチャンスを逃さないでください。

英語のウェブサイト

今ならあなたも英語のウェブサイトを読む事が出来ます。この作業を自分が楽し めるように、工夫して楽しいものにし続けてください。あなたが本当に好きな事の 情報をオンラインで探してください。

ネットにはたくさんの言語学習の情報があり、ネットサーフィンにより、自分の英語 を上達し続けられるにはどうすればいいか有効なヒントが見つかる事でしょう。こ れらのサイトから始めるのも良いかと思うので以下に記します。

www.talkenglish.com
www.englishclub.com
www.livemocha.com

あなたが私を信じて、この本をあなたの言語学習の手助けとして下さったことに対し、私 の心からの感謝の気持ちをここに表したいと思います。楽しい経験をされたならいいなと 思っております。

英語を話せる事はあなたの人生を大きく変える事が出来るという事を、私は本当に今は信 じています。

www.ingramcontent.com/pod-product-compliance
Lightning Source LLC
Chambersburg PA
CBHW060323070426
42446CB00049B/2012